NEW *ILLUSTRATED* ENCYCLOPEDIA OF GARDENING

UNABRIDGED

JAPANESE FLOWER ARRANGEMENT

CLASSICAL AND MODERN

By Norman J. Sparnon

Photography by Miki Takagi

GREYSTONE PRESS/NEW YORK · TORONTO · LONDON

To
my wife
Mary

Library of Congress
Catalog Card No. 60-9287

Greystone Edition Designed by Harold Franklin

Table of Contents

Forewords

By Sôfû Teshigahara, *Founder and Head, Sôgetsu School:*

Many persons from overseas have studied the art of flower arrangement in Japan. But none have attained the proficiency of Norman J. Sparnon. He holds the highest teaching rank of the Sôgetsu School and has entered his creations in more exhibitions in Japan than any other Westerner.

After many years of intense study, he is now publishing this book— a book I feel to be the most authoritative and beautiful ever published on this art. The reader is certain to find great joy and inestimable value in Mr. Sparnon's creativeness and the long years of artistic study that are embodied here.

I am strongly convinced that the publication of this book will have a profound effect upon the sound growth of the art of flower arrangement throughout the world.

Tokyo, Spring, 1960

By Tadao Yamamoto, *Director in Chief, Ikenobô School:*

Ikebana is a unique art that has been enriching and beautifying the lives of the Japanese ever since its origins in medieval Japan. This art that uses flowers as its medium is a manifestation of the love the Japanese have for nature and an expression of their longing for a peaceful life. My long-cherished desire has been that this art, the pride of Japan, could be introduced widely overseas. So I am deeply moved by the publication of this book on Ikebana by

Norman J. Sparnon, as it is so much in accord with what I have envisioned.

Mr. Sparnon came to Japan in 1945 and became interested in Japan's traditional art of flower arrangement. He was profoundly impressed by the harmony of tranquility and motion, the simplicity, and the oriental philosophy and atmosphere he found in the art. During the following twelve years in Japan he persevered in his efforts to attain a mastery of the art and has justly earned the title of *seikyôju*, the highest teaching rank of the Ikenobô School. Because of his superb artistic sense, his unremitting industry, and his profound love and true interpretation of the art, I feel sure that this splendid work of his will prove a brilliant success.

Speaking as one who bears the heavy responsibility of inheriting the Ikebana tradition authentically, imbuing it with new life, and transmitting it correctly to the younger generation, I sincerely hope that this book will be widely read in many countries and will give people throughout the world a true understanding of this Japanese art.

Kyoto, Spring, 1960

Author's Foreword

Steeped as it is in tradition, Japanese flower arrangement is apt to be considered a stereotyped though beautiful line-arrangement suited only to the austere simplicity of a Japanese interior. Nothing could be further from the truth. Were this so, the art would long since have been doomed.

Once the pastime of nobles and warriors, flower arrangement now constitutes an intimate part of the whole nation's culture. In the course of a long history it has developed along avenues of interpretation so numerous and diversified that its popularity today is unprecedented. So universal are the function and application of this art that few phases of Japanese life are untouched by its presence. It forms a field so vast and varied that no one individual could achieve mastery over the whole. It is by virtue of this universal appeal that the art has elicited the interest of flower-lovers the world over.

The present volume is a modest attempt to introduce the Western reader to classical and modern arrangements as exemplified by two of the largest and most reputed schools in Japan: the Ikenobô and the Sôgetsu. While the Ikenobô, with its history of more than twelve hundred years, is the oldest, the Sôgetsu, not yet forty years old, is one of the newest.

It is the author's cherished hope that this book may serve as a guide to those who are interested in Japanese flower arrangement and as a reference to those who have already studied the art. It is further hoped that the book will be received as a tribute to the masters of the Ikenobô and Sôgetsu schools, and that it will contribute toward the strengthening of the cultural ties between Japan and the Western world.

The author wishes to express his thanks to the following persons who by their teaching, advice, and encouragement helped make this book possible.

I am deeply grateful to Mr. Yûchiku Fujiwara and Mrs. Yoshiko Hosoyama, my teachers of the Ikenobô style, and to Mr. Sôfû Teshigahara and Miss Hakô Terai, my teachers of the Sôgetsu style.

I also wish to thank the following other members of the Kadô Kenkyûkai who assisted me in doing the *rikka* arrangements under the supervision of Yûchiku Fujiwara: Seikô Hara, Tadayasu Fujita, Yoshiko Hosoyama, Chitose Umeda, Yûko Tanaka, and Sadako Setoguchi.

For assisting me so ably in my historical research I wish to thank Miss Minobu Ôi, Professor of History, Women's University, Tokyo; and for his untiring assistance in translation work, Seiichi Miyazaki.

To Sen'ei XLV and Sôfû Teshigahara, the head masters, respectively, of the Ikenobô and Sôgetsu schools, I wish to express my appreciation for their arrangements appearing in this book as Plates 1 and 36.

To Miki Takagi, the well-known Tokyo photographer, without whose unstinting efforts and keen eye this book could never have been assembled, I am indeed most grateful. He took all of the photographs, both those of the author's arrangements and the other two mentioned above.

Finally, special thanks to Philip N. Jenner and Leo M. Traynor for their able editorial assistance.

Japanese Flower Arrangement

> *"If a man find himself with bread in both hands, he should exchange one loaf for some flowers; since the loaf feeds the body indeed, but the flower feeds the soul."* —MOHAMMED

Introduction

A Historical Summary

WHILE Japanese flower arrangement owes its origin to the introduction of Buddhism into Japan in the 6th century, as a studied form of art it may be said to date from the middle of the 15th century.

A legend which is still recounted by teachers of the older generation —a legend without mention of which no history of flower arrangement could be complete—is that of the Sun Goddess, Amaterasu-ômikami. Born from the left eye of the god Izanagi, Amaterasu received the land of Takama-ga-hara as her domain. Once, so runs the legend, she was visited by her unruly brother Susanoo-no-mikoto and became so outraged by his behavior that she fled into a rock cave and, sealing the entrance with an enormous stone, plunged the world into darkness. This caused great alarm among the other gods, who lost no time in formulating a plan to restore light to the world. One of them made a necklace of jewels, another a mirror; one fashioned certain hempen strips known as *nigite,* while another fetched a *sakaki* tree down from the heavenly Mount Kagu, placed it at the cave's mouth, and decked it with ornaments. Then one of the gods began to dance to the accompaniment of much music, continuing until Amaterasu, impelled by curiosity, peeped out to see what was going on. As she did so, the God of Strength reached in an arm, rolled the great stone away, and brought Amaterasu forth. Thus was light restored to the world. Susanoo-no-mikoto was banished to a distant region, where he overcame and slew the eight-headed serpent Yamata-no-orochi, in whose tail he found a sword, which he presented as a peace offering to his petulant sister. Whatever their origins, the sword, the necklace, and the mirror are to this day the three Sacred Treasures of Japan. The sword is enshrined in the Atsuta Shrine in Nagoya; the mirror has been in the Grand Shrine of Ise since the year 5 B.C.; the necklace is said to be kept in the Imperial Palace. The strips of hemp used in decoying Amaterasu out of the cave are now symbolized by the strips of paper, known as *shime,* that are hung in all Shinto shrines and can be seen during the many Shinto festivals throughout Japan. Branches of the *sakaki*—the Japanese character for which consists of the tree-radical plus the character *kami,* "god"—are to this day widely used in Shinto rites and as offerings before the small household shrines.

With such a tradition as this behind them, it is understandable how the Japanese could readily accept the idea of offering flowers to the Buddha. Though Buddhism was first introduced into Japan in the year A.D. 552, it was not until the reign of the Empress Suiko (593–628), who encouraged her nephew Prince Shôtoku in his efforts to establish the new faith, that it gained a permanent footing. In 607 one Ono-no-Imoko was dispatched as the first Japanese ambassador to China; it was apparently in China that this man gained a knowledge of the offering of flowers in the temples. On the death of his master and patron Prince Shôtoku, in 621, Ono-no-Imoko retired to a small priest's lodge *(bô)* near a pond *(ike)* on the grounds of the Rokkaku-dô, a small hexagonal Buddhist temple which Shôtoku had built in Kyoto. Taking the name of Senmu, he spent the remainder of his days praying for the repose of his master's soul and offering flowers before the six-handed Goddess of Mercy, guardian deity of Prince Shôtoku.

According to tradition, the people of Kyoto knew his place of retirement as the Ike-no-bô, meaning "the priest's lodge by the pond." The original structure is, of course, no longer in existence. The temple has been destroyed by fire several times and successively rebuilt. The present structure dates from 1877. In any case, the Rokkaku-dô has always been the residence of the head, and the headquarters, of the Ikenobô School of flower arrangement, which traces its beginnings back to the time of Ono-no-Imoko. The present head of the school is Sen'ei XLV, who succeeded to the title at the age of fourteen and is claimed to be the forty-fifth master in direct descent from Ono-no-Imoko.

There are no records of any systematized form of flower arrangement until the period of the civil wars in the late 15th century. The only materials that throw light on the forms in vogue prior to that time are *maki-e* (picture scrolls), embroideries, illustrated sutras, and poems. Those early arrangements, which may quite appropriately be termed prehistorical, fell into two classes: those which were used as Buddhist offerings, and those which were purely decorative. Both types were characterized by great simplicity. Floral offerings arranged by priests were to evolve from a primitive *tate-bana* ("standing arrangement") in a tall vase into the true *tate-bana* form later known as *rikka,* also meaning "standing arrangement." These last were highly stylized arrangements

Fig. 1. A single lotus flower and reversed leaf, symbolizing the positive *(yô)* and negative *(in)* principles of Oriental philosophy. Detail of an embroidery by an unknown artist, believed to have been presented in A.D. 925 by the Emperor Daigo to the Kanshû-ji temple, Kyoto, where it is still preserved.

Fig. 2. Detail of a stone bas-relief dating from 1306, now in the Museum of National Treasures, Kamakura, showing three-part symmetrical offerings before a *sanzon.*

which sought, through massiveness and elaborateness, to reflect nature's grandeur, might, and majesty; they no doubt developed hand in hand with the growing luxury of the nobility and to a lesser degree with the increasing magnificence of Buddhist temple interiors.

An embroidery believed to have been presented to the Kanshû-ji temple in Kyoto by the Emperor Daigo in 925 and still preserved there, depicts a slender vase containing one lotus leaf and flower held by a Buddha (Fig. 1). This simple arrangement is very interesting for the several basic principles which it embodies: the slender container; the leaf and flower rising as a single unit for a height of several inches from the mouth of the container; and the flower and the back of the leaf symbolizing the positive and negative principles of Oriental philosophy. The influence of this extremely simple form throughout the development of the classical arrangements is considerable.

During the Heian-Kamakura period (794–1333) there developed what is known as the *sanzon,* a characteristic representation in paintings, stone carvings, and the like of three human figures—one large central figure of a Buddha flanked by two smaller figures. Usually depicted near such groups are flower offerings, the three-part arrangement of which, consisting of one main stem with two shorter stems on either side, was apparently intended to echo the symmetry of the *sanzon* proper. A stone bas-relief dated 1306 and now in the keeping of the Kamakura Museum of National Treasures shows this form of offering (Fig. 2). The same form is also depicted inside the covers of the Itsukushima Kyôkan sutras dated 1163–69. Other three-branch arrangements were more consonant with the asymmetrical forms popular today. The celebrated Toba Sôjô Scroll (attributed to a monk of this name who died in 1114), depicting various animals arrayed in the vestments of Buddhist priests, shows a low taboret on which stands a tall vase containing an asymmetrical arrangement of three lotus flowers (Fig. 3). A *maki-e* or picture-scroll done in 1309 by one Takakane Takashina represents flowers in tall vases being used as room decorations (Fig. 4), and also shows two simple gatepost decorations. The famous Boki E-kotoba scrolls, dating from 1351, contain pictures of flowers in tall

FIG. 3. An example of an asymmetrical three-part offering of lotus flowers; a scene in the scroll attributed to the monk Toba Sôjô (died 1114), in the keeping of the Kôsan-ji temple, Kyôto.

FIG. 4. An example of a simple one-branch decorative piece, from a picture scroll by Takakane Takashina, dated 1309

vases together with candlesticks and incense burners, the whole arranged on a low table before pictures of Buddhas or founders of the Buddhist sects. Some of these arrangements are simple and straight; others, which appear to be decorative only, are done in the *nageire* style, characterized by a curved branch in a tall vase. Arrangements with candlestick and incense burner were of two styles, the *go-gusoku* and the *mitsu-gusoku,* and during the early period were the most widely used forms of floral offerings. *Go-gusoku* arrangements comprised an incense burner flanked by two candlesticks and two tall vases of flowers; *mitsu-gusoku* arrangements consisted of the incense burner flanked by a candlestick on one side and a vase of flowers on the other. This three-element combination began to be used purely for decorative purposes from the 14th century, and it was out of this type of floral offering that the *rikka* form developed. There is good reason to believe that while decorative pieces had previously been done in a kind of *nageire* style, floral offerings had been arranged in a proto-*rikka,* three-branch "standing" form. Another form of floral offering which obtained in the early period was the *sange* style, characterized by the placing of lotus petals in a container and sprinkling them before a Buddhist image or over the worshipers, and offering low, shallow containers piled with the heads of lotus flowers. This style of floral offering is believed to have been the forerunner of the 15th-century *rikka*-type arrangements in large shallow containers filled with sand, called *suna-no-mono.* The low tables on which arrangements are so often seen in the scrolls are known as *oshi-ita;* these are believed to have been the ancestor of the present *tokonoma* or ceremonial recess, incorporated into Japanese architecture in the late 15th century. This recess or alcove is an essential

FIG. 5. A *tokonoma* in which is displayed a *rikka* and a small *nageire* arrangement.

feature of every better-class Japanese home and is used for displaying art objects and flower arrangements (see Fig. 5).

From the colorful Muromachi period (1392–1490) the history of Japanese flower arrangement becomes a matter of written record. During this era of alternating civil strife and luxurious peace, culture reached a high degree of refinement. Flower-arrangement competitions are now mentioned for the first time, even though during this period more emphasis was placed on the container than the arrangement itself. Around the year 1470 a *rikka*-style arrangement in a gold vase by Sengyô (Senkei), the master of the Ikenobô School, created a sensation, and this date is now accepted as marking the birth of the true *rikka* style. In the priest Gekkei's preface to the *Hyakubinka-no-jo* by Senkei XXXI, an account of the exhibition of one hundred arrangements held at the Daiun-in temple in Kyoto in 1599, Sengyô himself is mentioned as the first Ikenobô master.

It was during the Muromachi period that the oldest document of flower arrangement, known as the *Sendenshô,* was written. According to a postscript, it was inherited in 1445 by one Fuami, then handed down to seven others, finally reaching the Ikenobô master Senji in 1536. As no Senji is listed in the genealogies of the Ikenobô masters, it is believed that he must have been Sennô XXVIII. The *Sendenshô* is a symposium of some fifty brief instructions on the arranging of flowers for various occasions. It names such forms as the "hanging boat" arrangement and the "post" or "pillar" arrangement, and specifies that the "boat" form is a *nageire* arrangement. The *rikka* form is mentioned among those based on the *mitsu-gusoku* type of arrangement. The only branch named is the *shin,* or "main branch," of a given arrangement, all others being referred to collectively as *soe-mono* or "supporting branches."

The development and great popularity of flower arrangement in Japan were due in large part to Yoshimasa Ashikaga (1435–90), the eighth Ashikaga shôgun, who was a patron of the arts. In 1478, after a somewhat turbulent life covering the Civil War of 1467–77, he built on a hill east of Kyoto a retreat which after his death came to be known as the Ginkaku-ji or Silver Pavilion. This structure, which still stands in Kyoto, is considered by many to be the birthplace of flower arrangement as well as of *cha-no-yu,* the tea ceremony. For ten years Yoshimasa lived in his Silver Pavilion surrounded by priests, poets, painters, and actors. One of the brightest stars of this galaxy was Sôami, a painter, poet, landscape gardener, master of the tea ceremony and of flower arrangement. Other eminent flower masters of the time were the samurai Hisamori Ôsawa and Senjun XXVI of the Ikenobô School. The accepted and popular form of arrangement at this time was the *rikka.*

But *cha-no-yu,* the highly refined ritual for preparing and drinking tea, was to play an important role in the further development of the art of flower arrangement. The tea ceremony had been brought to Japan from China, along with the Zen sect of Buddhism, by the celebrated priest Eisai (1141–1215); and in Japan the austere and simple Zen aesthetic developed its own equally austere and simple form of flower arrangement as a necessary adjunct to the tea ceremony. This new style, often consisting of but a single flower, is known as *chabana* or "tea arrangement." Sen-no-Rikyû (1520–91), regarded as the founder of the tea ceremony, was also a master flower arranger and is still known for his *nageire*-style arrangements of one flower. The *ichirin* or "single flower" arrangement is held to be a difficult accomplishment, and is a fundamental part of classical arrangements; to many it constitutes the essence of Japanese flower arrangement. It was from such simple arrangements, usually done in a slender container of medium height of bronze, porcelain, or bamboo, that the *nageire* and, later, the *shôka* styles developed.

The *Sanrei-ki* is a fourteen-volume diary and compilation by the court nobleman Yamashina and is now preserved in the Imperial Palace library. It includes eight volumes recorded by one of Yamashina's retainers, the warrior Hisamori Ôsawa, during the period from 1460 to 1492. These eight volumes, called the *Hisamori-ki,* form one of our chief sources of information on the types of flower arrangements then in vogue. It is in this work that we first encounter three well-known calligraphic terms (see pages 29–30 below) applied to flower arrangement—*shin* to arrangements in bronze containers; *gyô* to arrangements in shallow containers, then made of wood; and *sô* to "boat" arrangements. The *Hisamori-ki* also contains the first mention of bamboo containers of the type known as *take-no-tsutsu,* as well as of baskets, wooden buckets, and stone or pottery containers. This samurai flower-master arranged flowers at the palace and at the homes of the nobility. Although he neither founded a school nor trained students in his methods, after his death much of his style and many of his innovations were incorporated into the classical styles of arrangement. And it was during the opulent closing years of the 15th century, when Hisamori was working, the years known as the Higashiyama period, that flower arrangement became firmly established both as an art and as a pastime of the nobility. The civil wars which were to plague the country again from the early 16th century did little to retard its popularity.

There is no doubt that many forms of flower arrangement were in vogue at this time. For example, a scroll painted in 1529 by Gyokuka, a student of Ikenobô, depicts simple *rikka*-style arrangements, landscape arrangements, wall-type arrangements, "boat" arrangements, as well as arrangements in the *nageire* style. Nonetheless, it was the *rikka* form which was the most popular and which had caught the fancy of noble-man and warrior alike. The *Sennô-kuden,* written in 1542 by the Ikeno-bô master Sennô XXVIII, is a short treatise on the rules governing *rikka*-type arrangements as a mode of decoration. It gives the nomen-clature of the principal branches as *shin, soe, shin-i, mikoshi, nagashi-no-eda, mae-oki,* and *tai.*

By the middle of the 16th century the Rokkaku-dô had become renowned for its *rikka* arrangements by masters of the Ikenobô School. A picture scroll done by Sen'ami of the Ikenobô School in 1551 provides excellent examples of these early *rikka* arrangements. It illustrates the arrangements done for *mitsu-gusoku* as floral offerings and those made for the annual festivals (Figs. 6 & 7). Although different in style, they are relatively simple arrangements and are excellent examples of the forerunners from which the more massive and elaborate *rikka* arrange-ments were to develop. During the 16th and 17th centuries many works were written by successive Ikenobô masters on the development of the *rikka* form, and at the close of the 16th century this particular type of flower arrangement, which until then had been the pastime of priests, nobles, and warriors, became a profession.

The art's great popularity continued and was given even further im-petus by the Emperor Go-Mizu-no-o. By his command, the Ikenobô master Senkô XXXII was summoned to the palace, where an ex-hibition of *rikka* arrangements was held on July 7, 1629, with the emperor himself participating. This was the origin of the Ikenobô School's Tanabata-e, an exhibition held on the 17th and 18th of No-

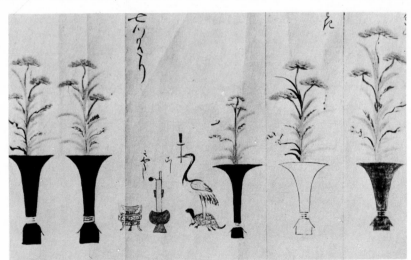

FIG. 6. Examples of typical early *rikka* floral offerings. The center panel shows the *mitsu-gusoku:* the incense burner (left), the candlestick (a crane on a turtle's back), and the flower arrangement. Between the incense burner and candlestick is a receptacle for implements used in handling the incense. Section of a picture scroll dated 1551, by Sen'ami, an Ikenobô master.

vember each year at the Rokkaku-dô in Kyoto, at which the leading teachers from all over Japan display their work. That exhibition at the Imperial Palace was unusual in not being limited to the nobility; indeed, this fact had a considerable effect in spreading the art to the lower classes. This circumstance, coupled with the great popularity of the art among priests, nobles, and warriors, made the 17th century the Golden Age of the *rikka* form.

In 1683 the five-volume *Rikka Taizen* or "Encyclopedia of *Rikka*" was published by Tauemon Jûichiya, a student of the Ikenobô master Senkô XXXV; this was the most complete study of the *rikka* form which had yet been made, and though altered by later masters, it still stands as one of the most outstanding and authoritative treatises on Japanese flower arrangement. While there were many prominent pupils of Senkô XXXV, there were also many deviationists. For example, eight volumes entitled *Rikka Imayô-sugata* or "Styles of Present *Rikka*" by Senkei Fushunken, dated 1688, show the amazing heterogeneity which prevailed. The best known of the deviationists who broke away from the school in Kyoto was Daijûin, who went to Edo (now Tokyo) and spread his art in that city. A volume published in 1679, containing illustrations of a hundred of his arrangements, shows his outstanding skill. One of his arrangements, done as a *suna-no-mono* in the Honnô-ji temple, is described as having been thirty-eight feet wide. The peak of massiveness in the *rikka* form was possibly achieved by the two arrangements on either side of the Great Buddha at Nara in 1693; each was forty feet high, their containers alone being seven feet high.

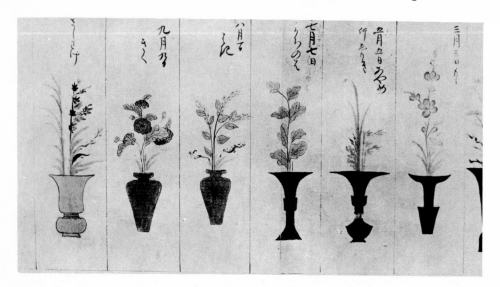

Fig. 7. Another section from the same scroll, showing examples of early *rikka*-style arrangements used for the five annual festivals. From right to left, the first arrangement (peach blossoms) is for Girls' Day, the second (iris) for Boys' Day, the third (*kudzu* vine) for Tanabata the fourth (bush clover) for the Mid-Autumn Festival, the fifth (chrysanthemum) for the Moon-Viewing Festival. The sixth piece, at the far left, is a double-*shin* arrangement.

A record of these arrangements is given in the supplement to the 1693 edition of *"Rikka Arrangements of the Rokkaku-dô Ikenobô and Its Disciples,"* originally published in 1674.

At the close of the 17th century political power began to shift from the military rulers to the merchant class, and with this transfer came a demand for a simplified *rikka* form. This was found in the asymmetrical *shôka* style, which had developed from the *nageire* and *rikka* styles early in the 18th century. The *nageire* form, which up to this time had included any type of arrangement other than those done in the *rikka* form, had evolved hand in hand with the tea ceremony and, together with the *rikka,* had enjoyed considerable popularity. The *shôka* form was based on three of the *rikka* form's principal branches— the *shin, soe,* and *nagashi,* which were renamed *shin, soe,* and *tai*—and combined the dignity of the *rikka* with the simplicity of the *nageire.* The anonymous *Nageire-bana Densho,* published in 1684, is a compilation of questions and answers on *nageire*-type arrangements done in various shapes of containers. Many of these—among others the basket, the square receptacle, the hanging and standing boat, the container with handles, the shallow container for shelves, and the two-level bamboo container—were incorporated into the classical *shôka* style.

The Ikenobô masters, who had excelled in the *rikka* form, had enjoyed a virtual monopoly in the domain of flower arrangement for many centuries. As a result, flower arrangement had become somewhat formalized and rigid. The new and simplified *shôka* style, however, offered limitless possibilities for variation, and as it spread to the masses, many masters broke with the old Ikenobô School in Kyoto and established styles and schools of their own. By the late 18th and early 19th centuries the *shôka* form had supplanted the *rikka* in popularity, and many different schools were in existence. Of these, the Ko-ryû, the Enshû-ryû, the Kôdô-ryû, and the Mishô-ryû schools are still flourishing. All of the new schools based their styles on the asymmetrical arrangement of three branches, as before, but introduced new angles for the placement of the branches and designated the branches by new terminology of their own choosing—such as *ten, chi,* and *jin* ("heaven, earth, man"), and *tai, yô,* and *tome.* Also popular around this time was the term *seika,* contrasting with the term *shôka* favored by the Ikenobô School. These two terms are simply different readings of the same two Japanese characters, which can in addition be read *ikebana*—the latter reading, not introduced until the late 19th century, being now synonymous with "Japanese flower arrangement," whereas the terms *rikka* and *ikenobô* had been applied to all forms of flower arrangement down to the appearance of the term *shôka.* In this connection, the term *heika,* literally "vase flowers," is synonymous with *nageire.*

Around the year 1820 a free-style type of arrangement known as the *bunjin-ike* was popularized by some of the leading artists of the day. This style followed no established school, but was instead a free expression of the arranger's own inspiration. Nevertheless, the trend to break away from the traditional styles was not to take firm hold until the 20th century.

With the establishment of the Meiji government in 1868, Western culture was brought into Japan along with hitherto unknown species of flowers, and this was to bring about a change in the style of arrangements. In 1887, flower arrangement was adopted as part of the school curriculum in many of the girl's schools and subsequently became part of the curriculum in all girl's schools until the outbreak of the Pacific War. With the inauguration of co-education in postwar Japan, flower arrangement no longer forms part of the public-school curriculum, but many private schools continue to offer it.

It may be mentioned here that the Japanese attitude toward flowers, as toward other manifestations of nature and toward esthetic interests generally, differs considerably from our own. The notion more or less prevalent in Western nations that the appreciation of floral beauty, or of nature itself, is necessarily a womanly weakness to which the male must never succumb, does not, and never did, obtain in Japan. It is somewhat paradoxical that, in this land of sexual inequality, nature and art should be admired by both sexes equally. Indeed, the art of flower arrangement has unquestionably been brought to its present high peak owing to the inspiration, the genius, and the leadership of men. Down to 1868 it was generally a man's avocation. Following the Meiji Restoration, and particularly after the beginning of the present century, flower arrangement was taken up by large numbers of women. Though men still head all the principal schools, it is safe to say that the art is now primarily in the hands of women.

An attempt was first made to utilize Western flowers in Japanese arrangements by Unshin Ohara, then an Ikenobô master, at an exhibition of the work of many schools held in Osaka in 1907. Since this necessitated certain changes in the *shôka* form of arrangement then in vogue, Ohara devised a new shallow container based on those used for dwarfed plants and tray landscapes, and set up a school of his own, since known as the Ohara-ryû. The great contribution of this school was the *moribana* form, a mode of arranging flowers in Ohara's new container which afforded greater freedom than had theretofore been possible in the selection and combination of flowers. As would be expected, this new form became immediately popular. From the *moribana* form arose the still freer *jiyû-bana* ("free arrangement") of the Shôwa era (1926 to date).

In 1930 the critics Shigemori and Fujii, together with the flower masters Teshigahara, Kuwabara, Yanagimoto, and Nakayama, proclaimed the birth of an advanced form of *ikebana* free of all ties with the past, which was later to become known as *zen'ei-bana* or "avant-garde arrangement." With war-clouds forming on the horizon, this advanced style was not to become popular until after the Pacific War. After 1945 it met with a prompt response on the part of the public and spread with astonishing rapidity. The guiding spirit of this new form of arrangement was Sôfû Teshigahara, who had founded the Sôgetsu School in 1926. Largely owing to the repercussions of his movement, all of the older schools, including the traditional Ikenobô, Enshû-ryû and Ko-ryû schools, now have their modern counterparts. In defiance of tradition, the Sôgetsu School made use of such apparently unpromising materials as iron, brass, stone, glass, vinyl, and plaster of Paris, previously unheard of as ingredients for flower arrangements. Under its leadership, *ikebana* became a creative, progressive art, devoted to the new, and thoroughly original in its conceptions. Highly controversial, the Sôgetsu School nevertheless thrived. Guided by men who skillfully adapted it to modern needs, it reached out and filled many a vacuum. Today, no longer confined to the home and studio, Sôgetsu arrangements are displayed for the pleasure of all in department stores, in the Kabuki, in cabarets, in public gardens, and over television.

Probably never before in its long history has Japanese flower arrangement enjoyed greater popularity than it does at present. Many hundreds of different schools have millions of students and teachers. Although no official figures are obtainable for the total number of schools, one authority's estimate is between two and three thousand. Of these, the Ikenobô, the Sôgetsu, and the Ohara schools dominate the scene. At the great national exhibits held annually in Tokyo and Osaka, thirty or forty different schools are represented; numerous exhibitions by individual schools are held throughout the year.

In retrospect, Japanese flower arrangement has passed through many phases since its inception over a thousand years ago. Today it is vigorous and progressive, as a living art should be, but any form of arrangement from any period of its history can be studied and practiced in present-day Japan.

Flower Arrangement in Japan Today

FLOWER arrangements in present-day Japan fall into three main types: those done in the home, those done in students' and teachers' study-groups, and those done for exhibitions. Despite their different ends, they have one important thing in common, namely the attitude of the arranger, for whom the utilitarian value of an arrangement is of much less importance than the satisfaction and spiritual exhilaration experienced in creating it.

Owing to the great number of apartment houses and the extremely crowded conditions of urban life, arrangements done for the home are nowadays usually in either the *nageire* or *moribana* styles or the more popular modern free style. In rural areas, however, the classical style is still popular. In many homes the use of flowers is restricted to the small household shrine; such a use does not in itself constitute flower arrangement, but in a sense it does play this role. In household Shintô observances small clusters of the leaves of the evergreen *sakaki* tree are placed on the high *kami-dana* or "god-shelf" together with the strips of paper called *shime* mentioned earlier in connection with the legend of Amaterasu-ômikami. Buddhists similarly employ small bunches of mixed flowers known as *kubana,* which developed out of the earlier *kuge* or "flowers for offering"; but though the art of flower arrangement owes its origin to such floral offerings, no attempt is made to arrange the *kubana,* which are bought ready-made from flower shops for a few yen.

It will perhaps come as a surprise to the Western reader to learn that the second type of flower arrangements in present-day Japan, those done in study groups, is the driving force of the art. From five to forty students, meeting together periodically, are usually provided by their teacher with containers and similar plant material; the work they do at these meetings is usually of a very high order. This is all the more true of the teachers' study groups. As many as a hundred teachers of one school gather at intervals under their head master, who provides them with like material and superior containers. Since the work done is criticized by the head of the school and, if need be, corrected by him, these meetings often result in outstanding arrangements. Considering that there are over one hundred thousand teachers in only two of the principal schools in Japan, one is justified in saying that there are very many such students' and teachers' study-group meetings every month.

The third type of arrangements, those made expressly for exhibitions, is a special category. Here the exhibitors do their utmost to create outstanding arrangements. Competitive exhibitions either within the schools or between the various schools are seldom held. The most important competitive exhibition held annually in Tokyo is the Ikebana Art Exhibition, where a panel of judges comprising both flower-masters and art critics judge the entries and awards are given in both fields. The most important non-competitive inter-school exhibition is the annual One-hundred-man Exhibition. This is participated in by one hundred selected masters of the various schools, one hundred in Tokyo and one hundred in Osaka. The various schools usually hold their own exhibitions once each year, and in addition to these annual events the larger schools ordinarily have exhibits of a week's duration in the great department stores, where thousands of people view their creations. As the space alloted to each exhibitor varies in width from two to nine feet, the opportunity presents itself for many large arrangements to be made. These large arrangements provide considerable scope for the exhibitor to demonstrate his creative ability. Quite out of place in the home, arrangements of this type are suitable only as decorative pieces in spacious areas.

Containers and Design

THE RELATIONSHIP between plant materials and container is a most important one in classical arrangements. As an old instruction book expresses it: "A good hand or a bad hand at flower arrangement is evidenced by the combination of flowers and vase." This has always been so in Japanese floral art; the container is not merely a vessel to hold water but an essential part of the total design.

From its earliest origins, Japanese floral art has been favored by a wealth of exquisite Chinese, Korean, and domestic containers of bronze, porcelain, and pottery. During the 15th century, in fact, more emphasis was placed on the container than on the contained, a circumstance undoubtedly due to the fact that flower arrangement, still in its infancy, was outshone by the highly developed art of the Chinese and Korean bronze workers and potters, who were exporting great quantities of their productions to Japan at that period.

As flower arrangement advanced, however, the emphasis on the container diminished until a better balance prevailed between it and the plant material, and the container became no more than a very important part of the arrangement as a whole. In modern Japanese arrangements the combination of flowers and container is no less important than in the classical schools, and the numerous potters of Japan are today producing excellent containers, some of which offer a real challenge to the arranger's ingenuity.

This refusal of the Japanese to subordinate the container to the contained does not mean, however, that a container is a necessary requisite to an arrangement; it means only that a container may make or mar an arrangement. In many modern arrangements no container is used at all, dried material being employed either alone or together with some non-floral object such as a wrought-iron piece. Sometimes, too, a small container is used but is entirely concealed by the plant material; in such an arrangement the container is not intended to play a part in the design.

When a container is incorporated into the design, as is usually the case, the arrangement may be likened to a symphony, in which the flowers are the musicians, the container the conductor, and the arranger the composer. All are individual artists in their own right, but perform together to produce a work of surpassing merit. The work will stand or fall according to the quality and harmony of its component parts.

Design is the most important factor in good flower arrangement, and the combination of flowers and container is a matter of design. Just as discrimination in the choice of parts enhances any design, so the selection of materials and containers which are in harmony with each other is essential to a well-designed flower arrangement.

Classical arrangements occupy a permanent place in the history of Japanese floral art and still have a universal appeal because of their beauty of line. Their variability of design, however, is far from infinite. At an early date, over-emphasis on design led to the formulation of rules so rigid that creativity was eventually shackled; this in turn led many masters to break away from the classical schools and to found schools of their own which encouraged free expression. Modern Japanese flower arrangement, as a result, is indeed infinite in its variability of design. The modern view is that rules should guide and assist, without impairing creativity. Design, instead of overshadowing the underlying idea of each arrangement, should be the vehicle of that idea. Hence an arrangement lacking good design communicates nothing to the viewer; it can never be more than a bowl of pretty flowers.

The flower arranger's task is primarily to enhance natural design or, stating the same idea another way, to compensate for nature's lack of design, by the well-considered placing, bending, and cutting of plant material; by the judicious combination of plant material with container; and, above all, by the proper utilization of space and the elimination of nonessentials.

This last point particularly deserves the attention of the student. To a Japanese master of flower arrangement, beauty may be achieved by creating space through elimination or placement; the basic idea is then presented simply and forthrightly, and is left to be accentuated by the space surrounding it. Here the Japanese masters excel. Their technique is perhaps best seen in the concept expressed by the term *shibui,* the "subtle simplicity" which pervades Japanese art in general. Such an employment of space naturally presupposes elimination, and where and what to cut is undoubtedly one of the most delicate aspects of flower arrangement. It is not easy, despite theoretical knowledge, to judge whether the space to be created by elimination is necessary or not.

A tree in foliage is a thing of great beauty; to the discerning eye it is no less beautiful, though in a different way, in winter when it stands bare. Seldom can a branch of any kind of material, however, be used in its natural form; each branch or flower must be carefully studied in order to utilize to the full its natural beauty. The camellia, one of the most difficult of all flowering plants to arrange effectively, is a good illustration. In its natural state, when in bloom, the tree is a mass of flowers and leaves. Cut a fairly long branch and observe it closely; it has a certain beauty of its own, to be sure, but from the standpoint of art it is just another camellia branch. Now take the same branch, remove all of its superfluous flowers, leaves and small branches; then, by careful bending, endow it with a pure line: you now hold an object of exquisite loveliness. There is frequent occasion to create design by the ultilization of space in mass arrangements, particularly in mass arrangements of a single kind of flower, where there is little variety of form. In this style of arrangement the emphasis must be on placement rather than elimination. This may be illustrated by an arrangement of sweet peas, which are characterized more by their beauty of color than by their beauty of line. Accordingly, when these flowers are massed they offer nothing but color unless they are carefully arranged, some tall, some short, and with space between them to create a design.

The beauty of individual flowers is attributable, in part at least, to their color, and beauty of color constitutes one of the pitfalls of flower arrangement. For color must be subordinated to design. An arrangement, which is good in design but poor in color combination may still be a good arrangement, while the converse is not true. This is brought out very strikingly by photography. A good arrangement will photograph very effectively in black and white, which ignores color entirely, while an arrangement strong in colors but weak in design will make a very poor black-and-white photograph.

The basic design in classical arrangements, whether *rikka* or *shôka*, is fixed, and though the arranger's role is simply to carry out this design, considerable experience and technique are required in order to do so. An analysis of the *rikka* will show the considerable thought that has gone into the planning of this handsome form of arrangement, both in the matter of design and in the combination of materials.

In modern arrangements the situation is somewhat different, for here the task is to realize one's own design, to carry it out within the framework of a basic pattern which serves as a rough guide to form, line, space, texture, and color harmony. In this resides the freedom of expression that has made Japanese flower arrangement the progressive art that it is today; and it is the competing creative force of several hundred schools that keeps the art progressive.

Part One

Classical Arrangements

~ 1 ~   Introduction

Classification of Plants

CLASSICAL flower arrangements are subject to strict principles governing the combinations of plants, the occasions when certain materials should be used, and the containers proper for specific plants and specific occasions. These rules are the cumulative result of studies made from the time of the earliest masters and have a purely esthetic rather than a botanical basis. It is this code of standards which has made Japanese flower arrangement what it is today, undoubtedly the most complete study ever made of floral art. At the same time, as previously stated, these same rules contained the seeds of their own breaking; for it was largely owing to their stringency that many teachers broke with tradition, thus creating the dualism which has made flower arrangement a virile, living, creative art. While, therefore, the possibilities of modern Japanese arrangements are limited only by the creative ability of the arranger, classical arrangements must still be done according to fixed principles.

The modern student may tend to disparage such rigid rules, but it should be kept in mind that they epitomize centuries of study and experience by men who devoted their lives and considerable talents to floral art, and that they have produced some of the world's masterpieces of flower arrangement. There can be no doubt that a mastery of such rules can do much to increase an arranger's technique even in the freest styles. The relationship is very similar to that existing between poetry in strict forms of versification and in the free forms.

The principles of classical arrangement can be best explained in connection with the traditional Japanese classification of plant materials. This classification reached its present form some two hundred years ago during the time of the Ikenobô master Senkô XXXV. Here we shall deal only with the general principles involved, taking up details as the occasion arises when discussing specific arrangements in later chapters. It will be necessary to use a few technical terms which may be unfamiliar, but these too will be explained in due course or may be found in the Glossary.

Plants, then, are divided into the two primary categories of *ki-mono*, "tree plants," and *kusa-mono*, "grass plants." In this classification, all woody plants are considered "trees," and all grasses and flowering plants are "grasses." Plants having characteristics of both categories are called *tsûyô-mono*, "common plants." This basic classification is recognized by all schools of flower arrangement, both classical and modern.

The further classification of plant material described hereafter pertains only to the *shôka* form, the simplified version of the *rikka*. In the *shôka*, secondary categories of plants are *ha-mono*, "leafy plants"; *mi-mono*, "berry plants," *tsuru-mono*, "vines"; and *tare-mono*, "hanging plants." Both the primary and the secondary categories of plants may, in addition, be subdivided into *oka-mono*, "terrestrial plants," and *mizu-mono*, "aquatic plants"; the former include woody plants, flowering plants, grasses, and "common" plants, while the latter comprise only flowering plants and grasses.

As a general rule, non-flowering material is not employed in *shôka* arrangements. It may, nevertheless, be used as one element of an arrangement. For example the pine, a non-flowering plant, is used extensively, but always accompanied by a *nejime*—a small cluster of flowers replacing the *tai*—and is never found alone. Flowering material, on the other hand, is often arranged alone. Certain materials such as silver willow, red osier, hazel, miscanthus, and burnet are not classed as grasses or flowering plants; these, therefore, must always be used with a *nejime* of flowers.

Such staple-cereal plants as rice, wheat, barley, oats, and rye are never used, either with or without a *nejime*. But other materials that were formerly also in the prohibited category are today sometimes used; these include plants bearing edible fruit, poisonous plants, sago palm, Japanese cedar, fan palm, Fatsia japonica, crape myrtle, and the trumpet flower.

KI-MONO OR "TREE PLANTS." "Tree" plants are characterized by beauty of trunk and limb, which when being arranged can be moulded into shapes evoking the line and mass of true trees; at the same time, their leaves and flowers (if such are present) enrich the completed arrangement in various ways. With the exception of those that put forth blossoms (e.g., plum, peach, cherry) and should be used only while in bloom, "tree" plants are suitable for any season of the year.

KUSA-MONO OR "GRASS PLANTS." In comparison with "tree" plants the "grass" plants are delicate, and this fact should be the first consideration in doing an arrangement. Practically all flowers are classed as "grasses." They may be arranged alone or used as a *nejime* with "tree" plants or, providing they are small, as a *nejime* with "common" plants. While the *nejime* almost always consists of flowers, non-flowering plants classed as "grasses," such as kale, may also be used. For an arrangement of "grass" plants a basket, pottery, porcelain, or bamboo container is preferable.

Tsûyô-mono or "common plants."　As we have already seen, "common" plants are those deemed to share the characteristics of both "trees" and "grasses," and are consequently treated as being weaker than "tree" plants but stronger than "grass" plants. Representatives of this category are bamboo, wisteria, peony, rose of Sharon, bush clover, spiraea, and hydrangea. When two different "common" plants are used in the same arrangement, one is treated as a "tree" the other as a "grass."

Ha-mono or "leafy plants."　All plants which are useful to the arranger more for the conspicuous beauty of their leaves than for their flowers are classed as "leafy" plants. Typical of this category are the aspidistra, banana, and lotus. The aster, hosta, Japanese iris, yellow day lily, and calla, notwithstanding the fact that they have flowers, are employed primarily for the beauty of their leaves. The maple, again, is essentially a "tree" plant, and like others of the category may be used together with flowers; but when its leaves take on their typical autumn colors, it is arranged alone. In such arrangements, the *shin* should consist of deep-red leaves, the *soe* of black-red leaves, the *tai* of red and yellow leaves; green leaves should be interspersed either in the lower part of the *tai* side of the arrangement or among the front leaves, or in both.

Mi-mono or "berry plants."　This category includes such berry plants as bittersweet, nandina, and Ilex serrata, but not species bearing edible fruits. In autumn and winter, when their berries are red, bittersweet and nandina are arranged with a *nejime* of small flowers; nandina is not used when it is in flower. Rhodea japonica is classed with the "berry" plants but is actually employed as a "leafy" plant.

Tsuru-mono or "vines."　Plants of this class are used only in hanging (wall, boat, moon) arrangements and for the upper level of double arrangements. Favorite materials are wisteria, bittersweet, and morning-glory. Materials which are not "vines" but which are also used in hanging arrangements are spiraea, yellow rose, and bush clover; these are classed as "hanging" plants.

TARE-MONO OR "HANGING PLANTS." This class, which is to be distinguished from the "vines," includes such plants as willow, bamboo, Japanese pampas, and bulrush; another member is broom. This material may be arranged with a *nejime* of flowers, though the latter should not be species belonging to this same class of "hanging" plants.

OKA-MONO AND MIZU-MONO OR "TERRESTRIAL AND AQUATIC PLANTS." As indicated above, certain species of woody plants, flowering plants, grasses, and "common" plants may also be classed as "terrestrial," while certain species of grasses or flowering plants alone may be further classed as "aquatic." A number of amphibious plants such as iris and reed, common to land and water, may serve now as "terrestrial" now as "aquatic" plants. The so-called "Fish Path" arrangement employs only aquatic plants, the "Water-Land" arrangement both a land plant and a water plant. Special rules governing these arrangements will be given later.

"In" and "Yo"

SOONER or later, the student of classical Japanese flower arrangement will be confronted with the terms *in* and *yô*. These are the Japanese readings of the same two characters which in Chinese are read *yin* and *yang,* the underlying meaning of which seems to have been "darkness" and "light" respectively.

In the dualistic, pre-classical philosophy of China, as expounded for example in the *I-ching* or "Book of Changes," *in (yin)* is the negative, passive, or female principle; *yô (yang),* the positive, active, or male principle. The phenomenal world is viewed as pervaded by these two contrary yet complementary forces: negative and positive are attributes of all things, some things being negative while others are positive. Ideally, there is a perfect balance between the two, for order reigns in the cosmos as long as the positive is in proportion with the negative, disorder accompanying the predominance of one over the other. Fortunately, both are capable of being manipulated by man (if he has the knowledge), and very often this is necessary. Indeed, harmony, good, success, and art can only be achieved through the controlled balance of these opposites.

Since the cosmos in all its aspects is made up of *in* and *yô,* it follows that, besides the values already ascribed to them, these terms are used to express many other paired associations. The chief of these are, in negative-positive order: black and white; evil and good; of ill omen and of good omen; foul and pure; weak and strong; left and right; moon and sun; and earth and heaven.

A glance at almost any form of plant life is enough to show that it grows upward out of the earth *(in)* toward the heavens *(yô)*. That part of the plant which faces the sun *(yô)* is held to be its front or positive side, while the part facing the dark earth *(in)* is its back or negative side. Whatever the student may think of *in* and *yô* as a *Weltansicht,* the careful discrimination and judicious balance of the positive and negative surfaces of plant materials constitute one of the fundamental secrets of successful flower arrangement.

It is with the *rikka* form, the fountainhead for all later schools of flower arrangement, that *in* and *yô* first appear as a systematized methodology in Japanese floral art. As we shall presently see, the *rikka* was an elaborate form of arrangement, often a veritable edifice of interrelated parts. Some way was needed for bringing order out of potential chaos, of balancing lights and shades, forms and lines, and individual parts in such a way as to create a perfect design. It was by applying the concept of *in* and *yô,* ready at hand in other fields of art, to flower arrangement that the *rikka* masters achieved their ideal.

How *in* and *yô* apply to flower arrangement can best be seen in the three-branch asymmetrical arrangements done in the *shôka* form. Here the primary *(shin)* branch ordinarily has a natural curvature, owing to its tendency during growth to bend towards the sun. Upon the orientation of the primary branch in the container depends that of the secondary *(soe)* branch. The direction in which the primary branch curves defines its *yô* (positive) side (see, for example, Plate 7), and the secondary branch must be placed accordingly. For example, if the primary branch curves to the viewer's left, the secondary branch will be placed to its left, with the *yô* side of the primary facing the *yô* side of the secondary branch. In this case the completed work is said to be a right-hand arrangement; this can be readily understood by viewing the whole from the standpoint of the primary branch itself—that is, by seeing it from the rear. Conversely, if the secondary branch (from the standpoint of the viewer) stands to the right of the primary branch, the arrangement is a left-hand one. An exception to this rule is when the positions of the secondary *(soe)* and tertiary *(tai)* branches are reversed, the former thus standing on the *in* side of the primary branch, the latter on its *yô* side; in such a case the secondary branch is known as a *gyaku-zoe* or "inverted *soe*" (see Pl. 28). As for the tertiary *(tai)* branch in the normal *shôka* arrangement, this must be so placed in the container that an imaginary line drawn from the secondary through the primary to the tertiary branch is straight; its *yô* side must face the *in* side of the primary branch. Owing to the fact that the three branches are in line and their axis set at an angle of forty-five degrees to the viewer, the arrangement manifests a balance and completeness which would otherwise be lacking.

The Three Styles

CLASSICAL arrangements, whether of the *rikka* or the *shôka* form, may be done in any of three styles, known as *shin, gyô,* and *sô*. These have sometimes been rendered as "formal," "semi-formal," and "informal" respectively. In reality, any arrangement done in one of these three styles, providing it adheres to the established rules, may be said to be a formal arrangement. In using English equivalents, the student is frequently hard put to dissociate from the intended meaning various unrelated notions inherent in the English; in view of this risk, we shall here employ the original Japanese terms and attempt to explain them.

As applied to styles of flower arrangement, the word *shin,* literally meaning "true," carries the idea of straightness or perpendicularity; the word *gyô,* meaning "moving," connotes moderate linear movement; the word *sô,* meaning "grass" (bending under the wind), connotes forceful linear movement. The same terms, deriving from calligraphy, are used with kindred values also in the seventeen-syllable verse form, the *haiku,* in painting, and in Japanese garden art. In brush writing, for example, the standard, carefully delineated block character *(shin-sho)*, comparable to our printed letters, contrasts with the mercurial "grass" character *(sô-sho)* or running hand, sometimes illegible yet always endowed with life, spirit, and great beauty. In between these two comes the versatile cursive character *(gyô-sho)*, sharing some of the qualities of both. In view of this close association with calligraphy, the terms straight, semi-cursive, and cursive have been extended to describe the three styles of *shin, gyô,* and *sô* as applied to floral art.

In the *rikka* form, the *shin* style is characterized by a straight primary branch, the *gyô* by a primary branch which curves somewhat to the right or left of the median axis. The *sô* style, on the other hand, is typically a low arrangement of considerable breadth, done in a wide, shallow bronze container filled with sand.

In the *shôka* form, the *shin* style is characterized by a primary branch which has a slight right or left curvature; arrangements in this style must always be made in a slender or narrow-mouthed container, such as one of bamboo (Figs. 8 & 9). In the *gyô* style, the curvature of the

FIG. 8. Three branches of pussy willow arranged in the *shin* or straight style.

FIG. 9. Typical containers for the *shin* style are, from left to right: *shikai-nami* "waves of the four seas"; *zundô* or *take-no-tsutsu,* bamboo container; *kanae-gata,* cauldron-shaped container; and *tsu-ru-ashi,* "crane's feet" or "standing crane."

FIG. 10. Three branches of pussy willow arranged in the *gyô* or semi-cursive style.

FIG. 11. Typical containers for the *gyô* style are, from left to right: *ogencho,* basket, and *usubata.*

primary branch is accentuated; this in turn calls for a wide-mouthed container such as an *usubata* or a basket (Figs. 10 & 11). The *sô* style is characterized by sweeping, free-flowing lines and is best suited to low, shallow containers, to certain kinds of bamboo containers, and to hanging arrangements (Figs. 12 & 13).

In both the *rikka* and *shôka,* finally, each style of arrangement is itself divided into *shin, gyô,* and *sô* sub-styles, giving a total of nine stylistic distinctions. Thus, an arrangement done in the *shin* style may, within the limitations set by the definition of this style, be relatively rectilinear (i.e., *shin* style, *shin* sub-style), relatively curvilinear *(shin-gyô),* or relatively sweeping *(shin-sô).* The sub-style is determined principally by the material, but also by the type of container, used. For clarity's sake, the classical arrangements in this volume are classified only according to style, no emphasis being placed on sub-style.

FIG. 13. Typical containers for the *sô* style are, from left to right: *suna-bachi* or sand bowl; *ichijû-giri* or one-level container, *tsuru-kubi,* "crane's neck"; and *nijû-giri* or two-level container.

FIG. 12. Three branches of pussy willow arranged in the *sô* or cursive style.

~ 2 ~ The Rikka Form

In ANY study of Japanese floral art the *rikka* form is necessarily mentioned as the most ancient systematized style of arrangement. Yet very little has been written on this form within recent times. *Rikka* arrangements—considered too complex, too time-consuming, too outsized for modern tastes—are commonly dismissed with the explanation that they were fostered by a more leisurely and opulent period of Japanese history and have no place in the art today.

Some of this is true and some of it is not. It is undeniable, for example, that the *rikka* form is difficult and requires serious study before the arranger achieves satisfactory results; it is also undeniable that *rikka* arrangements require considerable time and are ordinarily too large for the modern Japanese home.

Despite all this, as a studied form of floral art, the *rikka* is still supreme. From its origins in the 15th century down to the peak of its popularity in the late 17th century, it was practiced and recorded for posterity as no other form has been since. It was preferred to all others by priests, warriors, and nobles. It was the *rikka* form that inspired the magnificent, unprecedented exhibitions held at the Imperial Palace, in temples, and at the residences of the feudal lords. And finally, it is from the *rikka* form, ranging in height from a few feet to sometimes forty feet, that all present-day simplified forms of flower arrangement are descended, beginning with the asymmetrical *shôka* form in the early 18th century.

Not only is *rikka* a living art in Japan today, but its spirit pervades other more recent forms of flower arrangement. It is practiced both for its intrinsic beauty of mass and for the high degree of technical proficiency which it develops in the arranger—proficiency which may be translated into other forms of arrangement. *Rikka* arrangements are still to be seen at the great all-Japan exhibitions and at all exhibitions of the Ikenobô School. The contemporary *rikka* form, in which classical models provide the basis upon which the arranger improvises according to his free inspiration, occupies a permanent place in modern Japanese flower arrangement.

For the student of Japanese flower arrangement, therefore, the study of the *rikka* form will throw light on the origins of Japanese floral art; it will enhance his understanding of Japanese flower arrangement generally; and it will develop his technical ability in all forms of arrangement. One word of caution, however: the *rikka* constitutes a vast field of study and has been treated exhaustively by few authorities;

consequently, what is presented in this volume, though covering the rudiments set forth in Japanese texts and passed on by word of mouth from teachers to pupils, is necessarily limited.

The Branches and Their Positions

THE OBJECT of the earliest *rikka* arrangements was to awaken in the viewer the most elevated spiritual and esthetic emotions of which he was capable. The arrangers sought to accomplish this by suggesting to the viewer the ideal of sublimity, namely the mythical Mount Meru of the Hindu and Buddhist cosmology, known in Japanese as Shumi-sen. By means of plant life skillfully combined in a container, this form offered a symbolic representation centering on the sacred mountain but divided into seven distinct features as shown in Fig. 14:

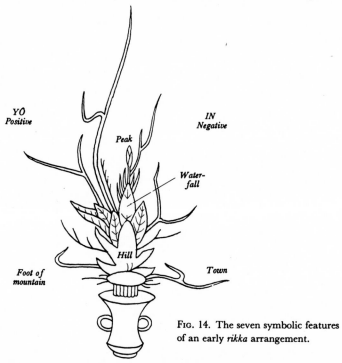

FIG. 14. The seven symbolic features of an early *rikka* arrangement.

(1) the peak itself, (2) a waterfall, (3) an adjacent hill, (4) the foot of the mountain, and (5) a town; the scene as a whole then being divided into (6) the sunlit or *yô* side, and (7) the shaded or *in* side.

The earliest reference to these seven features of *rikka* arrangements occurs in the *Sennô-kuden,* the oldest extant treatise on this form, published by the Ikenobô master Sennô XXVIII in 1542. Without expressly linking them with the seven features enumerated above, this work mentions by name the following branches: *shin, soe, shin-i, mikoshi, nagashi, mae-oki,* and *tai.*

From the middle of the 16th century the *rikka* form underwent successive modifications. The *Rikka Taizen,* published by Tauemon Jûichiya in 1683, names fourteen different branches, specifies the material to be used for each, and explains the role of each in the arrangement. Seven of the branches mentioned in this work are termed the *nanatsueda* or "seven principal branches"; these are the *shin,* the *shô-shin,* the *soe,* the *uke,* the *mikoshi,* the *nagashi,* and the *mae-oki.* The other seven branches are termed the "seven finishing places" of the arrangement.

By the time of the Ikenobô master Senjô XL (1786–1832) two other branches, known as the *hikae* and the *dô,* had taken on sufficient importance to be added to the so-called seven principal branches; the resulting nine branches came to be known as the *shichi-ku no dôgu* or "seven-nine branches," as seen in Fig. 15. It was during the time of this same Senjô that the principles of the *rikka* as we know them today were formulated. Whereas plant materials had previously been used

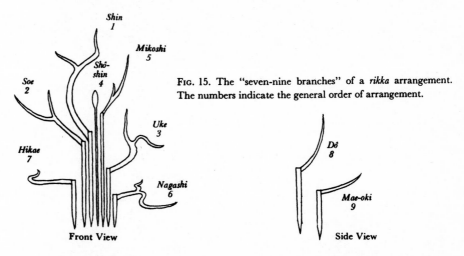

Fig. 15. The "seven-nine branches" of a *rikka* arrangement. The numbers indicate the general order of arrangement.

in their native state only, from Senjô's time branches began to be altered at will to obtain a desired shape.

In studying the *rikka* form it is advisable to use the original Japanese nomenclature for the branches rather than English substitutes, which are in some cases ambiguous or misleading. A list of the various branches with their approximate English meanings follows:

THE NINE PRINCIPAL BRANCHES

shin—"true, straight" branch
soe—"supporting" branch
uke—"receiving" branch
shô-shin—"perfectly straight" branch
mikoshi—"overhanging" branch
nagashi—"flowing" branch

hikae—"waiting" branch

dô—"body, trunk" of the arrangement

mae-oki—"anterior" branch

OTHER BRANCHES

ôha—"large leaves"

ushiro-gakoi—branches which finish the arrangement in the rear

ki-dome—the last "tree" material to be added

kusa-dome—the last "grass" or flower material to be added

ashirai—any supporting branch

The reader will observe that the position of the *soe* to the right or left of the *shin* determines the *yô* or positive side of the arrangement; this principle obtains in all forms of classical arrangement. It will also be remarked, in the sketch of a typical *rikka* arrangement (Fig. 14), that three large leaves *(ôha)* present their under *(in)* sides to the viewer while the two large leaves below the *soe* show more of their upper *(yô)* sides; the principle of employing one more negative *(in)* leaf than positive *(yô)* leaves is adhered to in all classical arrangements.

In the typical right-hand arrangement (that is, one in which the *soe*, from the viewer's standpoint, is to the left of the *shin)* the position of the various branches in the container is fixed. Their relative positions are shown in Fig. 16.

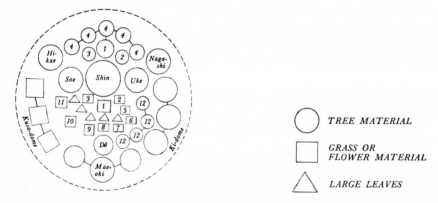

TREE MATERIAL

GRASS OR FLOWER MATERIAL

LARGE LEAVES

FIG. 16. Relative positions of branches in a typical right-hand *rikka* arrangement in which the *soe*, from the viewer's standpoint stands on the left of the *shin*. 1) The *shô-shin*. When this branch is of "grass" material *(kusa-mono)* it stands to the front of the *shin;* when of "tree" material *(ki-mono)*, to the back of the *shin*. 2) The *mikoshi*. When this branch is of "tree" material it stands to the right rear of the *shin;* when of "grass" material, to the right front. 3) The *uchi-zoe* or "supporting branch for the *soe."* When it is of "tree material," it stands to the left rear of the *shin;* when of "grass" or flower material, to the left front. 4) The *ushiro-gakoi*. 5–11) *Dô-uchi-no-kusa*. The path of the flowers from the right of the *shô-shin* down to the direction of the *hikae*. 12) *Iro-giri* (literally, "color cutting"). A "tree" material used to demarcate the *dô* and *mae-oki*, with which it contrasts, particularly when the *dô* and *mae-oki* are of the same or similar color material. Order of arrangement is from the *dô* to the direction of the *uke*.

A RIKKA arrangement done in the rectilinear *(shin)* style must have an absolutely straight *shin* branch. Though in *shôka* arrangements done in the same style the *shin* normally deviates from the vertical axis, it may not do so in the *rikka* form. The branch in question is therefore termed the *sugu-shin* or "straight *shin*."

In the curvilinear *(gyô)* style, on the other hand, the *shin* branch necessarily curves to the left or right of the arrangement's median axis; it is essential to note, however, that the upper extremity of the *shin* must return to that axis. The curvilinear *shin* is termed *noki-shin*, meaning "displaced *shin*"; this name it merits from the fact that—instead of following the arrangement's vertical axis throughout its length, as does the *sugu-shin*—it makes a detour, as it were, around the vertical axis, though its lower and upper extremities are on that axis. Given a *noki-shin* with a height of approximately six feet, the lower third of the branch consists of a base about four inches in height, above which is a two-foot section divisible into five equidistant levels, from any one of which the curvature of the *shin* may begin. This principle is illustrated in Fig. 17. Normally a *noki-shin* which branches out from the lower level will have a more pronounced curve than one branching out from the upper level. In the *gyô* style, therefore, the *shin* may be in the rectilinear or straight *(shin)*, the curvilinear or semi-cursive *(gyô)*, or the sweeping cursive *(sô)* sub-styles.

Rikka arrangements in the *sô* style are usually low and wide and are done in shallow bronze containers *(suna-bachi)* filled with sand; hence they are known as *suna-no-mono* or "sand arrangements."

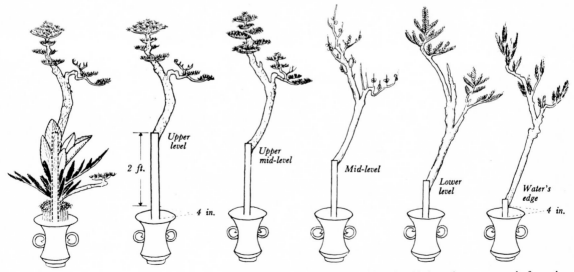

FIG. 17. The five levels from which the *shin* branch may protrude from the body of a *rikka* arrangement in the curvilinear or semi-cursive *(gyô)* style.

The Lengths of the Branches

THERE are no set rules governing the lengths of the principal branches. Ordinarily a *rikka* arrangement does not stand higher than six feet. (All height measurements given in this book include the container and, if used, the base on which it stands.) The height of the *shin* ranges from about three to five times the height of the container, depending on the material and the container being used. However, once the height of the *shin* is determined, all of the other branches conform to it according to an established pattern of proportions, illustrated in Fig. 18.

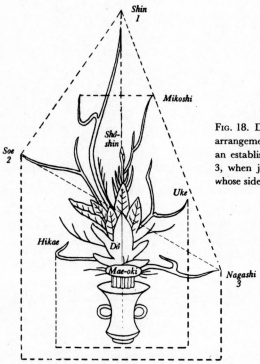

FIG. 18. Diagram illustrating how all branches of a *rikka* arrangement conform to the height of the *shin* branch in an established pattern of proportions. Points 1, 2, and 3, when joined by an imaginary line, form a triangle whose sides are all unequal.

It is on three of the main branches that all asymmetrical forms of Japanese flower arrangement are based. When the three-branch *shôka* form superseded the *rikka,* these branches came to be known as *shin, soe,* and *tai;* in the Sôgetsu School, to which the second half of this volume is devoted, they are termed *shin, soe,* and *hikae.* They are also known in some schools as *ten* (heaven), *jin* (man), and *chi* (earth).

As a general rule, no branch may protrude beyond the scalene triangle formed by the tips of the three branches, *shin, soe* and *nagashi.*

The *mikoshi* and the "supporting *shin*" branch are of the same height. The top of the *shô-shin* should rise slightly above the level of the *soe.* The *soe* and the *nagashi* should extend out to an equal distance from the arrangement's median axis; likewise, the *uke* and *hikae* should be equidistant from the axis.

Thus, if the *shin, soe,* and *nagashi* are removed, the arrangement is still a perfectly balanced one. It is still in balance if the *mikoshi, uke,* and *hikae* are removed.

From the tip of the *mae-oki,* which extends to the front, through to the back of the arrangement, the whole is nearly as deep as it is wide. The arrangement is thereby endowed with great depth, giving it a globular form.

Classification of Arrangements

THE STUDY of the *rikka* form is traditionally divided into six classes. These are: 1) Nineteen Styles, 2) Seven Forms of Study, 3) Three Forms of Okuden, 4) Komaki-den, 5) Ômaki-den, and 6) Variations.

The most fundamental and important of these classes is the Nineteen Styles, which is broken down into six groups:

1. Seven arrangements, each consisting of a single type of material—pine, cherry blossom, Japanese iris (Pl. 2), lotus (Pl. 3), chrysanthemum, maple, and narcissus.
2. Three arrangements in which the *dô* consists of pine, bamboo, or peony.
3. Three arrangements in which the *mae-oki* consists of pine, Rhodea japonica, or gleichenia.
4. Three arrangements involving the *nagashi:* a) *nagashi* and *uke* of the same material; b) *nagashi* protruding from the body of the arrangement and incorporating the *uke;* and c) *nagashi* appearing on the same side of the arrangement as the *shin* and *soe* (Pl. 5).
5. Two variations of the *shin* branch: a) a split or double *shin* (Pl. 4); and b) a *shin* comprised of two branches of young pine which when arranged appear as one. Both of these arrangements are straight arrangements.
6. An arrangement of azaleas known as *dan-no-tsutsuji,* named after a once-famous place in Kyoto.

Of the other five classes, the Komaki-den and Ômaki-den are not generally known. For those interested, the Seven Forms of Study and the Three Forms of Okuden are given in the Glossary (see *narai-mono nana-kajô* and *okuden san-kajô).*

FOR MORE than two hundred years the *rikka* style of arrangement reigned supreme as the popular choice of the Japanese nobility, the Buddhist priesthood, and the samurai class. This long period of popularity remains unprecedented for any one style of floral art.

The six styles of arrangements illustrated here have been selected from the Nineteen Styles of *rikka* with the exception of the *suna-no-mono* (Pl. 6), which is classified as a variation. Ranging in style from an arrangement of one kind of flower to an arrangement containing sixteen different kinds of material, they exemplify the great beauty and variety of styles to be found in this, the oldest studied form of floral art.

For the keen student a study of the *rikka* is an exhilarating experience. It is hoped that these arrangements will serve as a stimulus to those who are anxious to have a greater insight into the background of this fascinating art.

PLATE 1. LEFT-HAND NAGASHI ARRANGEMENT
BY SEN'EI XLV

Created by the head of the Ikenobô School at the Rokkaku-dô temple, Kyoto, the headquarters of the school, this arrangement beautifully . illustrates the variations which are possible in the *rikka* form.

This is called a left-hand *nagashi* because its *nagashi* branch appears on the positive side of the arrangement, the reverse of its normal position. From the position of the viewer, the left side of the arrangement is the side of the curve of the *shin* branch; this is the front or sun side of the branch and therefore the positive side of the arrangement.

Order of arrangement: The *shin* is the sweeping pine branch and is supported on the left by a branch of Japanese cypress. The *soe* is the long branch of Ilex serrata sweeping up to the top left; although it is much longer than the usual *soe,* here it provides a perfect balance between the *shin* and *nagashi.* The *uke* is the narcissus appearing on the top right under the *shin,* and is supported by the short branch of Japanese cypress. This position is usually the location of the *mikoshi* ("overhanging branch"). Due to the shape of the *shin* here used, such a branch would cut the *shin* line; therefore in this arrangement the *mikoshi* has

been incorporated into the *shin.* The *nagashi* is the branch of Japanese cypress trailing out to the left of the arrangement. The Iris japonica leaves appearing on the right of the arrangement are termed *honza nagashi,* meaning the "true position of the *nagashi.*" The *hikae* is the small clump extending rearward from the center of the Japanese cypress *nagashi.* The *shô-shin* is the straight branch of juniper centered under the *shin.* The *dô* or body of the arrangement is comprised of Ilex serrata backed with cypress branches. The *mae-oki* is the anterior branch of camellias. Irises appear on the lower right of the body of the arrangement. The "tree plant" *(ki-mono)* is represented by the branch of spindle tree under the *nagashi,* and the "grass plant" *(kusa-mono)* is the small chrysanthemums on the lower right under the iris leaves. The arrangement is rounded off with branches of young pine which are placed to the rear of the arrangement.

The arrangement is approximately six feet high, and stands in a partially glazed pottery container, on a red base known as a *kaban.* The drapes bear the crest of the Ikenobô School. The style of the arrangement is *gyô* or semi-cursive.

PLATE 1. LEFT-HAND NAGASHI ARRANGEMENT BY SEN'EI XLV

PLATE 2.   THE JAPANESE IRIS (IRIS LAEVIGATA)

FIG. 19. A straw base for this, as for all *rikka* arrangements, is made by tying straw very firmly into bundles and cutting lengths which, when fully inserted, will be about two inches below the container's rim. These lengths are then tied firmly together to make a bundle thick enough to fit very tightly in the container.

FIG. 20. Funnel-shaped holders and pipes, made of metal and covered with green paper, are usually used only for grass material or flowers. Material which is long and strong enough can be placed directly into the straw without such holders.

PLATE 2.   THE JAPANESE IRIS (IRIS LAEVIGATA)

Symbol of purity, innocence, and chastity, the Japanese iris, one of the seven plants arranged alone in the *rikka* form, has been used in classical arrangements for several centuries. Available during the four seasons of the year, it is widely used in all forms of Japanese flower arrangement. Its use in simplified form is covered in more detail in the following chapter. Dissimilar in construction to any other form of floral art, the arrangement presented here in pictorial sequence (Figs. 19–30) follows the basic pattern for all *rikka* arrangements.

The bronze container of the type known as *shiun* (literally, "purple cloud"), was introduced by a former head of the Ikenobô School. It stands on a red base called a *kadai*. The style of the arrangement is *gyô* or semi-cursive; it is a right-hand arrangement.

FIG. 22. The *shin* is placed in position in the tallest holder. It is supported by a flower to the rear and by two buds to the front and left. The leaf hanging to the right rear is the *mikoshi*. In an arrangement where heavy material such as pine is used as the *shin,* the pine branch would be fixed to a short stout piece of wood rather than to the funnel-type holder.

FIG. 21. The holders are placed in position in the straw base around a short length of wood to which they are tied in order to hold them firmly together.

Fig. 23. Leaves of the Iris japonica, which are wider than those of the Iris laevigata, are shown to the lower left of the arrangement. These are representative of the large leaves used in *rikka* arrangements. To the back, a leaf broken off by hand also appears in position. This is used for finishing off the rear of the arrangement. In arrangements of "tree material" (such as pine), young pine or juniper branches are used. This material is not placed in position until later in the arrangement; it has been shown at this point in order that their position may be clearly seen.

Fig. 24. The *soe* branch, consisting ▶ of two flowers, is added.

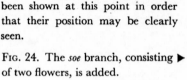

PLATE 3. THE LOTUS

Emblem of Buddhism, the lotus expresses many virtues: elegance, propriety, dexterity, purity, sincerity, and nobleness. An arrangement also symbolizes the three phases of existence: the past by the seed pod, the present by the open leaves and flower, and the future by the furled leaves and the bud.

This large, left-hand arrangement—so called because, when viewed from the rear, the *soe* (secondary leaf) appears to the left of the *shin* (primary leaf)—stands nearly six feet high, and consists of twenty-two leaves, one bud, one seed pod, one lotus flower, and three leaves and one flower of the yellow water lily.

The basic construction is the same as for the Japanese iris, all the material being held in position by funnel-shaped holders and pipes. In the simplified *shôka* form of this arrangement (Pl. 16), only one bud, pod, and flower are used, together with a minimum number of open leaves, usually only three or four.

The nine main branches and the order of arrangement are as follows: The *shin* is a large open leaf supported by a furled leaf to its left rear. The *soe* appears to the mid-right of the *shin;* it is a furled leaf supported by a pod, which inclines to the rear with its back or negative side to the viewer. The *uke* is placed to the left of the *shin* and is an open leaf supported by a furled leaf. The *shô-shin* is the straight bud supported by the partly furled leaf. The *mikoshi* is the tightly furled leaf appearing to the left of the bud. The *nagashi* is the furled leaf trailing out to the lower left. The *dô* is the furled leaf with its back or negative side to the viewer, and the flower and the furled leaf facing the viewer. The *hikae* is the open leaf to the lower right under the pod, while the *mae-oki* is the large open leaf which extends horizontally toward the viewer. The *ki-dome* or "tree plant" is the tightly furled leaf to the lower right; the *kusa-dome* or "grass plant" is represented by the two leaves and flower of the yellow water lily on the lower left of the arrangement. At the back is placed a partly withered leaf which is used to round off the arrangement.

The bronze container, known as *sonshiki-gata,* meaning "ladle shaped," stands on a red base called an *usuban* and a black base called a *kaban.* The style of arrangement is *gyô* or semi-cursive.

PLATE 3.   THE LOTUS

PLATE 4.   DOUBLE-SHIN ARRANGEMENT

FIG. 25. The *uke,* also consisting of two flowers, is placed to the right.

FIG. 26. The *shô-shin,* consisting of two buds, is placed in the same holder as the *shin.* The *nagashi,* consisting of one bud, trails out to the lower right. When it is necessary to bend the stem at an acute angle, a piece of wire is inserted up through the stem, or the wire is covered with green paper and affixed to the under part of the stem.

FIG. 27. The *hikae,* consisting of one flower, is placed to the left under the *soe.*

PLATE 4. DOUBLE-SHIN ARRANGEMENT

This divided arrangement, constructed from sixteen different kinds of material, gives the appearance of one arrangement split in two.

Of the nine principal branches it features two primary branches together supported by one *soe, uke, mikoshi,* and *hikae,* and two *shô-shin, nagashi, mae-oki,* and *dô.*

Order of construction of the left side of the arrangement: The tall primary branch *(shin)* is cypress. The *soe* is the long branch of Ilex serrata on the upper left supported by one branch of the Japanese yew and a branch of juniper. The *nagashi* is the long branch of pine trailing out to the left with the *hikae,* a branch of pine, appearing above the *nagashi* to the left rear. The *shô-shin* consists of the two chrysanthemums directly under the *shin.* The *mae-oki* and *dô* are comprised of box interspersed with a branch of the spindle tree. The large leaves are three loquat leaves, two negative and one positive. Below the long branch of pine at the lower left, the "tree plant" is represented by the rose, and the "grass plant" by the small chrysanthemums. Chrysanthemums are placed throughout the body of the arrangement. The left side of the arrangement is com-pleted by placing long branches of young pine to the rear.

Order of construction of the right side of the arrangement: The *shin* is the tall branch of pine, the *uke* the branch of pine to the mid-right supported by a branch of the Japanese yew. The *mikoshi* ("overhanging branch") is the long branch of Ilex serrata between the two branches of pine; it too is supported by a branch of Japanese yew. The *nagashi* is the trailing branch of Ilex serrata to the lower right which is supported by a branch of juniper. The *shô-shin* is the celosia directly under the pine *shin.* The large leaves are represented by the broad leaves of the Iris japonica appearing under the celosia. The *dô* and *mae-oki* are branches of azalea leaves interspersed with a branch of the spindle tree. The "tree plant" and "grass plant," placed under the *nagashi* branch of Ilex serrata, are represented by the camellia and gentian. The right side of the arrangement is also completed by placing long branches of young pine to the rear.

The height of the arrangement is approximately six feet. The style is *sugu-shin,* meaning "perfectly straight."

◀ FIG. 28. The *dô*, consisting of two buds and two flowers, is placed in the midfront of the arrangement.

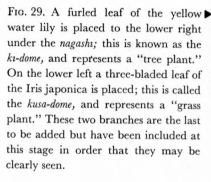

FIG. 29. A furled leaf of the yellow ▶ water lily is placed to the lower right under the *nagashi;* this is known as the *ki-dome,* and represents a "tree plant." On the lower left a three-bladed leaf of the Iris japonica is placed; this is called the *kusa-dome,* and represents a "grass plant." These two branches are the last to be added but have been included at this stage in order that they may be clearly seen.

PLATE 5.   LEFT-HAND NAGASHI ARRANGEMENT

This arrangement features the *nagashi* branch (the branch of juniper trailing out to the lower right) on the positive side of the arrangement, the reverse of its normal position. It will be noted that in the left-hand *nagashi* arrangement of Plate 1 the *nagashi* is on the left, whereas here it is on the right; in both arrangements, however, it is on the curved side of the primary branch *(shin),* which is the positive side of the arrangement. The name left-hand *nagashi* is therefore a little confusing, for whether it is on the left side or the right side of the viewer, so long as it is on the same side as the curve of the *shin,* which is also the side of the *soe,* it is always termed a left-hand *nagashi.*

The order of arrangement is as follows: The *shin* is the large branch of juniper dominating the arrangement. The *soe* is formed of the five branches of pussy willow appearing on the upper right-hand side. In a usual *rikka* arrangement the *soe* plays a more important role, but when the *nagashi* branch is featured on the positive side of the arrangement, the *soe* is usually subordinated to it. Below the pussy willow, a short branch of Japanese yew supports the *soe.* The *uke* is the large juniper branch on the left of the arrangement. The *shô-shin* is comprised of the two chrysanthemums in the top center, and the *mikoshi* is the long branch of Ilex serrata inclining to the top left. The *nagashi* is the long branch of juniper trailing out to the lower right, and into it is incorporated the *hikae.* The branch of Ilex serrata appearing above the *nagashi* supports the latter. On the left side of the arrangement, directly opposite the *nagashi,* appear three short branches of pussy willow; these branches are termed *honza nagashi,* meaning the "true position of the *nagashi.*" The *dô* or body of the arrangement and the *mae-oki* or anterior branch are made up of enkianthus leaves. As they are of the same material, they are cut by a small branch of the spindle tree. The large leaves or *ôha* are loquat leaves, of which there are two negative and one positive. Small chrysanthemums comprise the "grass plant" appearing under the *nagashi,* and the three roses on the lower left side represent the "tree plant." The arrangement is rounded off with tall branches of young pine placed at the rear of the arrangement.

The height of the arrangement is approximately six feet. The large bronze container known as *rikka-hei hôô-mimi-tsuki* (literally, "a *rikka* container with phoenix ears attached") is restricted to *rikka* arrangements. The style is *gyô* or semi-cursive.

PLATE 5. LEFT-HAND NAGASHI ARRANGEMENT

PLATE 6.   ARRANGEMENT IN SAND

PLATE 6. ARRANGEMENT IN SAND

An arrangement made in sand is always broader than it is high, and is always arranged in a large, shallow container. Although it is called a "sand arrangement" *(suna-no-mono)*, the method of construction is the same as for all *rikka* arrangements. The branches and, whenever necessary, the funnel-type holders are placed in the usual tight straw base (Figs. 19–21) which is fitted into a hole in the center of a board. The board rests approximately one inch down from the top of the container and is covered with sand. This cursive arrangement, with its broad, sweeping lines, together with the straight *sugu-shin* and the semi-cursive left-hand *nagashi*, clearly illustrates the three styles of arrangements termed *shin*, *gyô*, and *sô*.

Order of arrangement: The *shin*, *soe*, and *nagashi* are the sweeping branches of podocarpus. One branch comprises the *shin* and *soe*, with the *shin* trailing above the center of the arrangement. A branch of Japanese yew supports the *soe*. The *nagashi* trails out to the left. The *uke* consists of the two branches of Ilex serrata appearing to the mid-left. The *mikoshi* is the branch of willow extending from the top center and is supported by a branch of Japanese yew. The *shô-shin* is the straight branch of Ilex serrata directly under the *shin*. The *hikae* is the branch of Ilex serrata on the lower right and is supported by a chrysanthemum. The *dô* and *mae-oki* consist of box and are cut by the branch of spindle tree. Chrysanthemums are placed throughout the body of the arrangement. The "tree plant" is represented by the branches of sago palm appearing on the left under the *nagashi*, and the "grass plant" by the small chrysanthemums on the lower right. Branches of young pine finish off the arrangement at the rear.

The width of the arrangement is approximately seven feet.

The bronze container is a *suna-bachi*, meaning a "sand bowl," which was originally introduced for this type of arrangement. The plain wooden base is known as an *usuita*. This is a left-hand arrangement. The style is *sô* or cursive.

FIG. 30. The arrangement is completed (see also Pl. 2) by adding the anterior branch known as the *mae-oki*, which extends to the lower front. It consists of two flowers and five leaves of the yellow water lily. In this part of the arrangement this material is preferred to iris, but if iris is used it should consist of one or two large flowers.

As MENTIONED previously, the *shôka* form developed out of the older *rikka,* of which it is a simplification. Like all other forms of Japanese flower arrangement, irrespective of period and school, it is an asymmetrical form built up from three principal branches of unequal lengths. These branches are called the *shin,* the *soe,* and the *tai* and are the counterparts, respectively, of what are commonly known as *ten, jin,* and *chi* ("heaven, man, earth"). The *shin* is the primary branch, the tallest of the three; the *soe* the secondary branch, of intermediate height; the *tai* the tertiary or supplementary branch, the shortest of the three.

The height of the *shin* above the water-level may be from one and a half to three times the height or width of the container, depending upon the container, the type of plant material, and the location of the completed arrangement. The *soe* should be two-thirds the height of the *shin;* the *tai,* one-third the height of the *shin.* These proportions endow the arrangement with three levels—upper, middle, and lower. The upper level comprises the *shin* or the *shin* group of branches; the middle level, the *soe* or *soe* group of branches; the lower level, the *tai* or *tai* group of branches.

By *"shin"* group of branches and the like is meant the *shin* branch taken together with one or more of the *ashirai* or "supporting" branches, leaves, or flowers which may be added to it. For the number of such supporting branches that may be used there is no fixed rule; apart from the dictates of the plant material itself (which will be discussed when describing specific arrangements), this decision is left to the discretion of the arranger. The proportions of the *ashirai* are, however, subject to rules.

When one or more *ashirai* are used with a principal branch, these decrease successively in height by intervals of about ten percent of the height of the *shin.* Thus, the first supporting branch for a thirty-inch *shin* would be twenty-seven inches high; the second supporting branch, twenty-four inches; the third, twenty-one inches; and so on. With a thirty-inch *shin,* the *soe* should be about twenty inches high; consequently its first supporting branch would be about seventeen inches high, the proportion still being reckoned from the *shin* rather than from the *soe.* Hence the *tai,* ten inches high for a thirty-inch *shin,* would require its first supporting branch to be seven inches high.

Of the three branch groups just described, the *tai* and its supporting branches call for special attention. Whereas the *shin* group and the *soe* group both decrease regularly, when the *tai* group consists of more than two branches it forms a "valley." In such a case the branch (within the *tai* group) lying nearest to the *shin* is designated *tai no shin,* that is, the "*shin* branch of the *tai* group"; and though the single *tai* branch is normally one-third the height of the *shin,* the *tai no shin* may be as much as half the height of the *shin.*

In the *shôka* form the *shin* branch is curved; it should curve to the left rear or to the right rear, depending on whether the arrangement is a left-hand or a right-hand one. If the branch is divided into five equal parts, it will be found that the maximum curvature falls within the second fifth from the bottom. The top of the *shin* should be in line with its base, and the horizontal expansion of its curve should not pass beyond the outer edge of the container.

The position of the *soe* or secondary branch is indicated by the curvature of the *shin;* if the latter curves to the left rear (the viewer's left), the *soe* is placed to the left rear of the *shin,* and conversely. The *tai* or

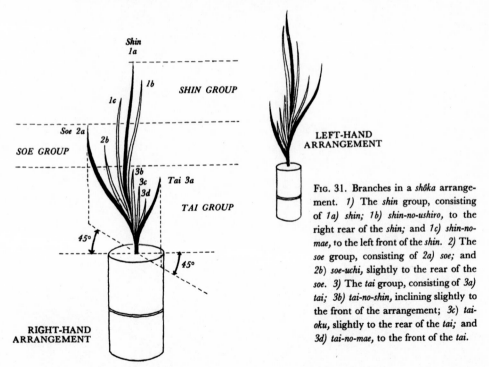

Fig. 31. Branches in a *shôka* arrangement. 1) The *shin* group, consisting of *1a*) *shin;* *1b*) *shin-no-ushiro,* to the right rear of the *shin;* and *1c*) *shin-no-mae,* to the left front of the *shin.* 2) The *soe* group, consisting of *2a*) *soe;* and *2b*) *soe-uchi,* slightly to the rear of the *soe.* 3) The *tai* group, consisting of *3a*) *tai;* *3b*) *tai-no-shin,* inclining slightly to the front of the arrangement; *3c*) *tai-oku,* slightly to the rear of the *tai;* and *3d*) *tai-no-mae,* to the front of the *tai.*

tertiary branch is placed to the right or left front of the *shin* in line with the *soe.* Thus, looking down upon a *shôka* arrangement, an imaginary line drawn from the *tai* through the *shin* to the *soe* would be perfectly straight. The same line would, moreover, lie at an angle of forty-five degrees from the left-to-right axis of the arrangement in such a way as to be oblique to the viewer (Fig. 31). Also, now looking at the arrangement from the front, the angle at which the *soe* and *tai* incline from the arrangement's vertical axis is the same, the specific degree of the angle depending on the style *(shin, gyô,* or *sô)* in which the arrangement is done (Figs. 8, 10, 12) and also, of course, on the type of plant material and the container.

The curve of the *shin* branch marks its front, positive, or sun *(yô)* side, which is also the side of the *soe.* Its back, negative, or dark *(in)* side is the side of the *tai* branch. The front of the *soe* is placed so that it faces the front of the *shin,* while the front of the *tai* faces the back of the *shin.* In this way the front of the *soe* and the back of the *tai* are always toward the viewer of the arrangement. The positive or *soe* side of an arrangement, incidentally, is known technically as the *shimo-za* (literally, "lower seat") or "host's place," while the negative or *tai* side is known either as the *kami-za* (literally, "upper seat") or the *kyaku-i* (literally, "guest place"), both meaning the seat of honor. There is an exception to the rule that the *soe* marks the positive *(yô)* side of the arrangement: the position of the *soe* and *tai* may be reversed, in which case the resulting arrangement is termed a *gyaku-zoe* or "inverted *soe"* arrangement (see Pl. 28). In this type of arrangement the positive and negative sides are the same as described above; that is to say, the curvature of the *shin* still indicates the positive side.

Plant material is held fast in the container by one of several primitive clamp known as *hana-kubari* (see Fig. 32). Of these the most common types are the forked twig *(matagi)* and the crossbar *(ichi-monji).* Whatever the number of branches in the arrangement, the plant material should rise as a single stem, devoid of foliage to a height of about four inches above the container's mouth—this latter being known as the *mizu-giwa* or "water's edge." With the exception of those made in baskets, *shôka* arrangements are usually displayed on a low table (Pl. 20) or on a plain or scrolled base (Pl. 7).

In conclusion, it should be pointed out that classical arrangements are based on general rules recorded in the *densho*—a series of documents drawn up by former masters of the Ikenobô School which, collectively, may be considered the bible of this school. Various interpretations of these writings, however, may be made by different masters, resulting in some slight variations in the styles of arranging.

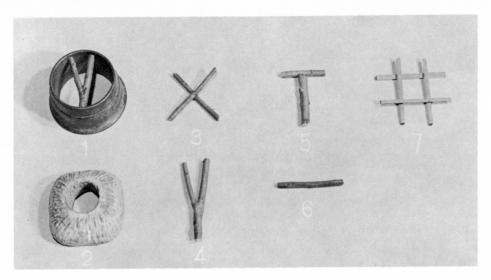

FIG. 32. Various types of *hana-kubari*. The forked twig *(4)* and the simple crossbar *(6)* are the most commonly used. *1* and *2* are used with arrangements done in the cursive *(sô)* style, in low, shallow containers. *3* to *6* are used both for the straight *(shin)*, the semi-cursive *(gyô)*, and the cursive *(sô)* styles. *3, 5,* and *6* are used in narrow-mouthed containers, such as those of bamboo. *7* is used with an arrangement of pine, bamboo, and plum, or of peonies.

～5～ *Shoka Arrangements: Plates 7-35*

THE ARRANGEMENTS presented here are considered fully representative of this simple three-branch asymmetrical form which developed from the *rikka*. Although arranged in accordance with definite rules and to a set pattern, they are sufficiently diversified to illustrate the beautiful designs which can be achieved by the combination of plant materials, containers, and bases.

The student should pay careful attention to the third dimension, which is so important in all styles of Japanese floral art. In the classical style the arrangement always stands or hangs obliquely to the viewer.

Many of the classical arrangements illustrated here can be done very effectively in shallow contemporary containers with a needle-point holder. Similarly, plant material other than that called for by the classical rules may be used quite successfully, a practice known as *gendai-ka,* or "modern flowers," and widely followed in Japan today. In these adaptations of the classical arrangements it is usually necessary to conceal the needle-point holder under crushed rock or pebbles.

PLATE 7. THE CHRYSANTHEMUM

Symbol of immortality and also the imperial emblem of Japan, the chrysanthemum is available throughout the year in numerous colors and varieties; it is undoubtedly the most widely used flower in the land. This simple arrangement of three chrysanthemums illustrates the basic asymmetry of all Japanese flower arrangements and is a clear example of the pattern common to all the classical arrangements in this book.

The length of the primary branch *(shin)* is approximately twice the height of the container. A stem with a natural curve has been selected, with the flower almost directly in line with the base but inclined as though looking toward the sun.

The secondary branch *(soe)* follows the line of the main branch but leans to the left rear; its flower is turned toward the *shin.* The front or positive side of the *soe* faces the positive side of the *shin.*

The tertiary branch *(tai)* leans to the right front with its back or negative side to the viewer and its head turned slightly toward the *shin.*

All three branches are located on a single plane intersecting at an angle of forty-five degrees an imaginary line drawn from the viewer through the center of the container. The three branches rise as one stem and are free of foliage for a height of about four inches above the mouth of the container. The leaves should not cut the line of any of the flowers and should not droop. The three flowers are held in place by the forked-twig *kubari* (Fig. 32, No. 4), which is placed firmly in position about one-half inch below the mouth of the container. Water should just cover the *kubari.*

The order of arrangement is *tai,* then *shin,* and then *soe.* The three-legged bamboo container known as *kanae-gata* ("cauldron shaped") stands on a scrolled base called *maki-dai.* This is a right-hand arrangement *(hon-gatte)* done in the *shin* or straight style.

Chrysanthemums are arranged in odd numbers, usually from three to fifteen. An exception is an arrangement of two chrysanthemums, with the second flower being used for either the *soe* or *tai,* or merely as a supporting flower for the *shin.* In the latter case chrysanthemum leaves are used for the *soe* and *tai.*

PLATE 8. THE ASPIDISTRA

Aspidistra leaves are the most important basic material in the study of classical arrangements and by far the most widely used among the leaf plants. A mastery of the arrangement of these leaves means almost certain success in the arrangement of all other classical material. They are arranged alone and in odd numbers from three to fifteen leaves. An exception to this rule is when two leaves are used with a *nejime* of small flowers.

In arranging aspidistra there are certain basic rules which must be followed. First, the leaves must be divided into two groups, those which are wider right of center and those which are wider left of center. As explained before, the front of a flower or leaf is the positive side and the back is the negative side. In addition to this, with the aspidistra the wide side of the leaf is also positive and the narrow side is negative. Irrespective of the total number of leaves used in an arrangement, the number of leaves placed in front of the *shin* must always equal the number to the rear. The positive side of the arrangement as a whole is the side on which the secondary leaf *soe* appears. Therefore, each leaf must be oriented in such a way that its positive or wider half is in accord with the orientation of the arrangement as a whole.

In the arrangement of nine leaves illustrated here, and numbered in Fig. 34, the *soe* (8) appears on the right and the *tai* (1) on the left. There are four leaves in front of the *shin* (5) and four leaves to the rear. All leaves in front of the *shin* and the *shin* leaf itself are negative leaves and therefore must be placed with their backs to the viewer in order that the wider portion of each leaf will be oriented correctly with the positive side of the arrangement (1–5). All leaves to the rear of the *shin* are positive leaves since the wider half appears right of center when viewed from the front (6–9). The main leaf *(shin)* forms the center of the arrangement, and the front or positive side faces to the right. Since it is a negative leaf, most of the back is turned to the viewer; however, a portion of the front should also be visible. The point of the lower left leaf *(tai)* is turned down to show part of the positive side. The secondary leaf *(soe)* is a positive leaf and therefore shows its positive side.

All the leaves other than the *shin, soe,* and *tai* are termed supporting leaves or *ashirai.* Of these, the three leaves (2–4) in front of the *shin* show their backs or negative sides. The leaf (7) to the left of the *soe* shows

a lot of the positive side. The tall leaf (6) to the left rear of the *shin* is turned down to show both sides. The small leaf (9) gives support to the *tai* and shows a lot of the positive side.

To sum up, all positive leaves show their fronts, and all negative leaves, their backs. The *shin,* being the central and principal leaf, shows both.

This arrangement is a left-hand *(gyaku-gatte)* arrangement. A comparison with the previous arrangement of three chrysanthemums will show that the complete arrangement has been reversed.

The height of the *shin* leaf is approximately two and a half times the height of the container; the *soe,* two-

◀ FIG. 33. The three main leaves are shown separately. The *tai* (left) and the *shin* (center) are negative leaves, and when viewed from the back, the wider portion of each will be seen right of center. The *soe* (right) is a positive leaf; when viewed from the back, the wider portion is left of center.

FIG. 34. The white dot indicates the wider ▶ side of each leaf. The numbers indicate the order in which the leaves should be arranged.

thirds the height of the *shin;* and the *tai,* one-third the height of the *shin.* It should be noted, however, that because the *tai* leaf hangs down it is fore-shortened; therefore, it is better to make this leaf a little longer than one-third.

The bamboo container is called a *zundô* or *take-tsutsu;* it stands on a scrolled base. The style of the arrangement is *shin* or straight.

For a five-leaf arrangement, leaves numbered 1, 4, 5, 6, and 8 are used. Leaf No. 6, to the back of the *shin,* would be approximately five inches shorter than the *shin,* and Leaf No. 4, to the front of the *shin,* would be approximately half the height of the *shin.*

For a seven-leaf arrangement, leaves numbered 1, 2, 4, 5, 6, 7, and 8 are used. Leaf No. 6 would be approximately five inches shorter than the *shin,* and Leaf No. 4 would be approximately five inches shorter than No. 6.

PLATE 9.   ASPIDISTRA LEAVES AND SMALL CHRYSANTHEMUMS

This right-hand arrangement of two aspidistra leaves with a *nejime* of small chrysanthemums illustrates an exception to the rule that aspidistra leaves are arranged alone. A *nejime* is a small group of flowers which takes the place of the *tai* and is used when there are no flowers in the *shin* or *soe* groups. As a general rule, in such an arrangement the *shin* and *soe* will be leaves or some other evergreen material.

In this arrangement the length of the *shin* leaf is about two and one-half times the height of the container; the *soe,* two-thirds the length of the *shin;* and the tallest of the flowers, one-third the length of the *shin.* Since this is a right-hand arrangement, the *shin* leaf when viewed from the front is wider right of center, and the *soe* leaf is wider left of center. In this way the two leaves are in perfect harmony, the wide portion of one leaf being opposite the wide portion of the other. This is the same principle as outlined in the previous arrangement of aspidistra leaves. The *shin,* being a negative leaf, has most of its back turned toward the viewer with only a small portion of the front or positive

side showing at the top. The *soe,* being a positive leaf and also the positive pole of the arrangement, reveals more of its front or positive side.

The *nejime* is itself a complete arrangement in miniature. Although the little group of flowers as a whole comprises the *tai* of the greater arrangement, this group has its own asymmetrical form. The tallest flower is placed in front of the *shin* leaf. The *tai* of the miniature group, which is the flower nearest to, and inclined toward, the viewer, is roughly the same length as the tallest flower in the *nejime,* but as it projects forward, it appears shorter when viewed from the front. The shorter flowers are placed between these two stems.

The order of arrangement is first the *tai* of the *nejime,* followed by the short flowers, the tall flower, the *shin* leaf, and finally the *soe* leaf.

The two-legged bamboo container is called *tsuru-ashi* ("crane's feet") or *tachi-zuru* ("standing crane"). The style of the arrangement is *shin* or straight.

Fig. 35. The three groups of leaves after they have been reconstructed. From left to right: *tai, soe, shin.*

PLATE 10. NARCISSUS

An arrangement of narcissus is subject to special rules governing the leaves, the flowers, and their placement in the container. As in iris arrangements, emphasis is placed on the leaves, which must be taken apart and reconstructed to achieve the desired effect.

In this right-hand arrangement three groups of leaves and flowers have been used. The length of the *shin* is approximately twice the height of the container; that of the *soe,* two-thirds the length of the *shin;* and that of the *tai* point (that part of the *tai* group extending farthest forward), one-third the length of the *shin.* Either two or three groups of leaves and flowers may be used. If two groups are used, one is for the *shin* and *soe* and the other for the *tai.* One group of leaves and flowers must always consist of four leaves and one stem of flowers. As the leaves usually grow in groups of from four to six they must be taken apart. This is accomplished by slightly squeezing and removing the small sheath which holds the leaves and flower together at the base of the stem. Care should be taken not to break the sheath, as leaves have to be reinserted in it. Four leaves are then rearranged as indicated in Fig. 35.

The two outer leaves enclose the two inner leaves. It is easier to place the leaves in the sheath one at a time. The flower, being in the middle, is inserted last. The point of the sheath should be turned toward the viewer, and when placed in the container it should be visible just above the lip of the container. For this reason it is necessary to place the sheath three or four inches up from the base of the stems. The *tai* flower should be either a bud or a half-open flower. The *shin* flower should be open. The flowers may be either odd or even in number.

Order of arrangement in the container is first the *tai,* then the *soe,* and then the *shin.* If only two groups are used, the *soe* leaves must be placed in front of the *shin* leaves. This rule of placing the *soe* between the *tai* and *shin* is an exception to the general rule.

The style of arrangement is *shin* or straight.

The narcissus is one of the seven flowers to which the Ikenobô School has traditionally given particular attention. The other six are the banana leaf, lotus, Rhodea japonica, camellia (one-flower arrangement), peony, and morning-glory.

PLATE 11. WEEPING WILLOW AND NARCISSUS

This one-level arrangement, commonly known as *ichijú-giri*, is correctly termed *ryôsô-ike*, meaning an arrangement in two windows. It earns this title from the fact that the container is open on both sides.

The *shin* is the long branch of willow, a little less than twice the height of the container. The *soe* is the lone branch trailing out to the left, approximately two-thirds the length of the *shin*. The *tai* is the narcissus, the long leaf of which is one-third the length of the *shin*. In this arrangement it is important that the material should not touch the sides of the window. Also, the *tai* side of the window should not be crossed by any of the *tai* leaves or flowers. The top of the *shin* should not hang directly over the top of the container, and the distance between the *shin* and the edge of the container should be more or less equal to the diameter of the container.

The arrangement of the two clusters of narcissus is the same as for the narcissus arrangement of the previous plate.

This right-hand arrangement is held in place by a forked twig in a bamboo container known as *ryôsô* or *ichijú-giri*. The plain wooden base is the *usuita*. This style of arrangement is always *sô* or cursive.

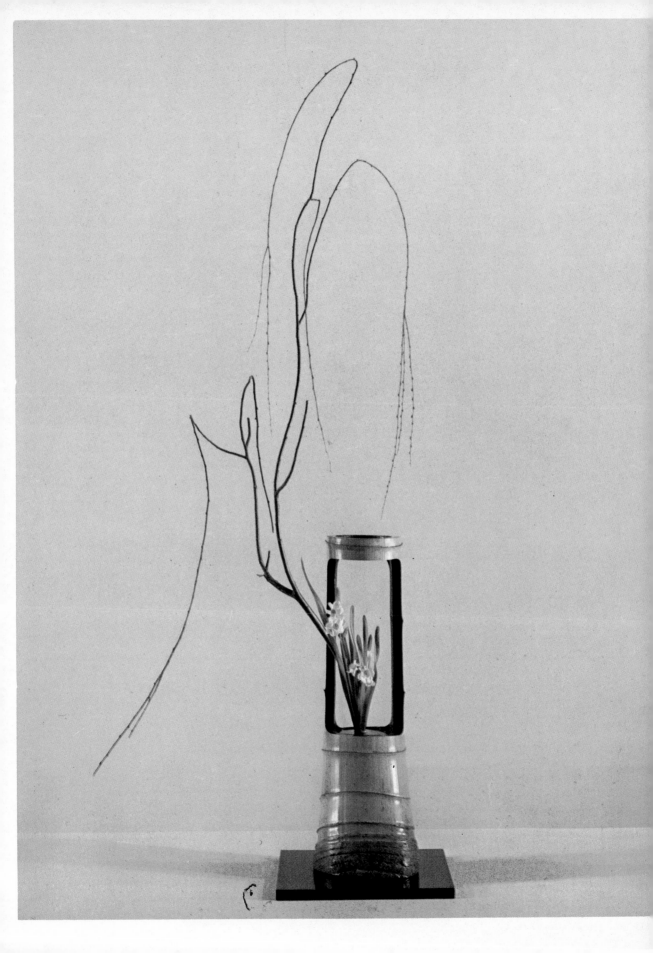

PLATE 12. CELASTRUS, CHRYSANTHEMUMS, AND STONECROP

With very few exceptions, classical arrangements contain only one or two kinds of material. The exceptions are the traditional New Year's arrangement of pine, bamboo, and plum (Pl. 34); the Seven Grasses of Autumn (Pl. 31); and double, or two-level arrangements, such as that illustrated here.

In this basic double arrangement the *shin* and *soe* appear on the upper level, the *tai* on the lower level. The *shin,* the long branch of celastrus, hangs down the side at approximately forty-five degrees to the front to about the middle of the window. The *soe,* which is always of the same material as the *shin,* trails over the top of the container. The stonecrop, which comprises the *tai* on the lower level of the container, is placed at an angle of about forty-five degrees to the right shoulder. The top of the *tai* should never reach beyond the top of the container, nor should any part of it touch the window. The small *nejime* of chrysanthemums on the upper level completes the arrangement.

In double arrangements either two or three kinds of materials may be used, but never more than two varieties of flowers. The material on the upper level should differ from that on the lower. An exception to this rule is that the Japanese iris may be used without any other material on both upper and lower levels. Either level of the container may be used alone, but the unused one should be filled with water, and only one or two varieties of material may then be used.

The material used for the *shin* in the top level may be hanging material, such as celastrus, morning-glory, or wisteria; material with a less definite tendency to hang, such as knotweed, lythrum, or spiraea; or material such as the Japanese iris, cryptomeria, or juniper, which does not hang at all. Hanging material should hang down to about the middle or just below the middle of the window. The second variety may extend to just below the level of the top of the container. The third variety should not reach below the level of the top of the container.

The container, which is known as a *nijû-giri,* stands on laced bamboo. This style of arrangement is the basic double right-hand arrangement or *nijû-ike-no-hanagata* and is always *sô* or cursive.

FIG. 36. The fork of the *kubari* is placed well to the back of the container. This enables the stems of the star lilies to rest against the wall of the container and so lean forward.

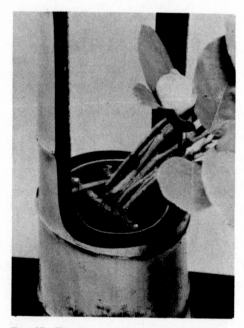

FIG. 37. The branches of magnolia rest on the base of the container and are held firmly in place by two *kubari:* the forked twig and the crossbar *ichimonji.* Water just covers the top of the forked twig in both the upper and lower levels.

PLATE 13. MAGNOLIA AND RED STAR LILIES

This double, left-hand arrangement in the climbing style differs from the previous arrangement in that the *shin* and *soe* appear on the lower level and the *tai* on the upper. Nevertheless, each level has its own three-branch form. The *shin,* approximately one and one-half times the height of the container, is placed at an angle of approximately forty-five degrees and extends toward the right or left shoulder to a point above the container. On the lower level the *shin* and *soe* are each a branch of magnolia; the *tai* is a single bud. On the upper level the *shin, soe,* and *tai* are all red star lilies. It is important that the branches do not touch the sides of the container; in particular, the *tai* leaves or flowers should not touch the frame of the window. In the arrangement illustrated here, the left side of the window is clear. It is also important that the *shin* should cross the side of the window a little below the center.

This style of arrangement is the double climbing style called *nijû-tachinobori-ike.* It is always *sô* or cursive.

PLATE 14.   THE CAMELLIA

The arrangement of a single flower, known as an *ichirin,* is probably one of the most beautiful of all Japanese flower arrangements. Since the origin and spread of flower arrangement in its studied form in the 15th century and the adoption of a flower arrangement as one of the accessories of the tea ceremony for which Zen Buddhism demanded austere simplicity, one-flower arrangements have always formed and still form an important part of both classical and contemporary styles.

The arrangement of a single flower is considered a difficult accomplishment, and a good arrangement never fails to arouse the admiration of all devotees of Japanese floral art.

The arrangement of a single flower with a table and an incense burner originated some five hundred years ago during the Muromachi era. After the introduction of the *tokonoma,* a tall table was introduced to hold an incense burner; the incense implements were placed in a small container on the lower shelf. These implements were soon replaced by a small, simple arrangement of flowers, which is believed to be the origin of the popular *nageire* form of arrangements. One of the old forms of decoration in a large *tokonoma* was for the table to be flanked by two *rikka* arrangements in front of four hanging scrolls. When *shôka* replaced *rikka* as the popular form of arrangement, the table, the incense burner, and the flower were incorporated as one of the classical forms.

This left-hand arrangement of three and a half camellia leaves and a flower exemplifies the natural asymmetrical form of the *shin, soe,* and *tai* to be found on a single branch. *Shin* is the tall leaf; *soe,* the leaf to the right; and *tai,* the single flower and two leaves. The positive and negative principle of *yô* and *in* have been carefully applied to enhance the beauty of the arrangement. The *shin* leaf is turned to show both its front and back, and both the *soe* and *tai* leaves are turned down. The *soe* has the appearance of a half-leaf. In this way the arrangement, although small, has both balance and depth. If all the leaves were vertical and faced the viewer, the arrangement would be flat and uninteresting. Tradition demands that this arrangement consist of one flower and three and a half leaves. The half-leaf may be naturally broken, broken by hand, or turned to appear as a half-leaf.

This one-flower arrangement uses one of the seven traditional flowers of the Ikenobô School and is now recognized as the most important of all single-flower arrangements.

The flower is held in place by a small forked-twig *kubari* and is always in the *shin* or straight style. The container, which measures five inches in height, is of old Chinese jade.

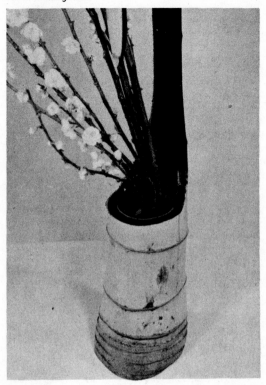

PLATE 15. PEACH BLOSSOMS

The third day of March is Girl's Day in Japan, and dolls reminiscent of ancient court life are elaborately displayed in the homes and department stores during this festival. No display, however modest it may be, is complete without an arrangement of peach blossoms, the traditional flower for this occasion.

This right-hand arrangement of peach blossoms has been made in an interesting bamboo container called *tsuru-kubi,* "crane's neck." The length of the *shin* is one and one-half times that of the container. In this arrangement the secondary branch *(soe)* has been placed in front of the *shin* and projects to the left front instead of to the left rear. The *tai* inclines to the right front. This is contrary to the general rule and is known as *mae-zoe,* meaning "*soe* to the front."

The style of arrangement is *sō* or cursive.

68   *Classical Arrangements*

PLATE 16. THE LOTUS

Emblem of Buddhism and symbol of purity and immortality, the lotus is used in arrangements to depict the three phases of existence: the past is represented by the seed pod; the present, by the open leaves and the flower; and the future, by the furled leaves and the bud.

An arrangement usually consists of three or four open leaves, a variable number of furled and semi-furled leaves, one flower, one bud, and one pod. The total number of leaves is usually even, while the total number of leaves and other elements is usually odd. The use of the floating leaf is confined to lotus arrangements; the container must of course have a wide mouth.

In this right-hand arrangement the *shin* is approximately one and one-half times the length of the container and is supported by the semi-furled leaf, the seed pod, and the bud. The *soe* is a semi-furled leaf. The *tai* is the open leaf, the flower, and the small furled leaves.

The important features of an arrangement of the lotus are as follows: The *shin* should be an open leaf. Semi-furled leaves are placed to the center, but it is common practice for the *soe* to be an open leaf. A bud is placed in the center or upper part of the arrangement, and the flower and a withered or open leaf in the lower part. The pod should be placed to the side, and furled leaves at the water's edge. The floating leaf should be small. The lotus is always arranged alone and is not used on felicitous occasions.

The bronze container is the *suna-bachi,* which is filled with sand when used in a *rikka* arrangement (Pl. 6). The style of arrangement is *sô* or cursive.

PLATE 17. SPIRAEA

There are three boat arrangements, each depicting a stage in the voyage of a boat: incoming, outgoing, and in port. This right-hand arrangement of trailing spiraea is an outgoing *(debune)* arrangement. In this form the long trailing branch symbolizes an oar and is used in addition to the regular *shin, soe,* and *tai*. Its length may be up to approximately one and one-half times the length of the boat; it should always trail down toward the viewer. The *shin* is about half the length of the oar; the *soe* is two-thirds the length of the *shin*. The *shin* and *soe* represent the sail of the boat; they should not touch or cross the suspending chains. The tip of the *shin* should be directly under the apex formed by the three chains. The *soe* should be to the left rear.

The prow of the boat should always be to the left, and the curve of the *shin* and *soe* should always billow toward the prow. The *shin,* the *soe,* and the oar usually consist of the same material. A small *nejime* of different material may be used at the base of the arrangement to divide the *shin* and the trailing oar.

The *irifune* arrangement depicting an incoming vessel is not illustrated here, but it is just the reverse of this arrangement. The prow faces to the right, and the oar trails to the left. Both *irifune* and *debune* arrangements, collectively known as *tsuri-bune* (hanging boat), are always hanging arrangements, with the water in the boats not visible. They are always done in the *sô* or cursive style. The in-port arrangement is shown in Plate 19.

FIG. 39. A small forked twig holds the branches in place. Placing the fork to the rear of the container makes it easier to hold the long trailing oar in position.

PLATE 18. THE MORNING-GLORY

The hanging moon arrangement known as *tsuri-zuki* has two forms: the half moon and the full moon. The *shin* may either hang down or trail out to the side, according to the type of material.

In this right-hand arrangement the long trailing *shin* is approximately twice the width of the container. The *tai* is the flower; the *soe*, the leaf above the *tai*. The *tai* flower is supported by the tendril to its side. The *shin* should cross the container at an angle of approximately forty-five degrees. When the morning-glory is arranged, a short length of bamboo is used to support the *shin* at the mouth of the container, and the *tai* is an open flower. This form of arrangement does not require that the stem of the material be clear of the container.

In moon arrangements the *tai* is always inside the moon. The *soe* may be either in or outside. If it is inside, the tip of the *soe* should be under the chain; if outside, it should not cross the chain.

The moon may be arranged with two kinds of material, but if morning-glory is used, it is usually arranged alone.

This style of arrangement is always *sô* or cursive.

PLATE 19. THE JAPANESE IRIS

After the chrysanthemum, the iris is probably the most popular flower in Japanese flower arrangement; and yet, with its many varieties and the many complicated rules governing its use, it is possibly one of the most difficult for the beginner to arrange. The most important feature of any iris arrangement is the leaves, and a few general words should be said here concerning the leaf shapes of the different varieties before considering this specific arrangement.

The chief varieties of iris used are Iris laevigata or the Japanese iris, Iris tectorum, and Iris ensata, each of which has a differently shaped leaf. The center blade of the three leaves of the Iris laevigata is the shortest. With the Iris tectorum the three blades increase in length from left to right. The center blade of the Iris ensata is the tallest of the three.

In any classical arrangement only the *tai* leaves, which are those nearest the viewer, retain their natural form. All other leaves are arranged in units either of a single blade or of two blades. To get the proper leaves for a good arrangement it is necessary to pull the leaves

apart and then reconstruct them. Great care must be used to reconstruct them correctly, an operation to which the Japanese pay particular attention.

The order of reconstruction may be understood by reference to the figures on page 100. All these illustrations are for a right-hand arrangement; for a left-hand, the position of the blades would be reversed. The hooked tips of each pair of blades and of the outside blades of a three-bladed leaf should turn inward; the tip of the center blade of each triplet should face to the left. (For a left-hand arrangement it would face to the right.) It will be noted that in each illustration the pair of leaves on the right is the tallest, and the pair in the center is the shortest. This is the general order of arrangement for iris leaves.

To return to the present arrangement, the tall, straight leaves of the iris—in this case Iris laevigata or the Japanese iris—are particularly appropriate for such an arrangement as this, known as a *tomari-bune* or *oki-fune* and depicting a boat in port.

When using material other than the Japanese iris

FIG. 40. THE JAPANESE IRIS (IRIS LAEVIGATA). The three-bladed leaf on the left is to be used for the *tai;* the long blade is to the right front; the short blade, to the center rear. In the two-bladed leaf in the center the longer blade is to the right front. In the two-bladed leaf on the right the longer blade is to the left front.

FIG. 41. IRIS TECTORUM. The leaves of this iris are arranged in the same manner as for the Japanese iris with the exception of the *tai* complex, which retains its natural gradation in length from left to right. The leaves of the Iris japonica and Iris nertschinskia are arranged in the same manner as the Iris tectorum.

FIG. 42. IRIS ENSATA. For this the longest blade of the three-bladed *tai* complex is placed to the center rear, with the second longest blade to the right front. For the two-bladed leaf in the center the shorter leaf is placed to the left front. For the two-bladed leaf on the right the shorter leaf is placed to the right front. (This placing of the short blade over the long blade is just the opposite of what is done with the Iris laevigata and the Iris tectorum.)

for this arrangement, two varieties may be used, but one is preferable. The length of the *shin* is usually one and a half times the length of the boat. However, since in the arrangement shown here the boat is rather large, the *shin* is approximately the same length as the boat. The open flower and the three-bladed leaf comprise the *tai;* the two leaves and the bud are the *shin;* and the *soe* is a single leaf. There is one additional leaf, to the right rear of the arrangement, which gives support to the *shin.* The tip of the taller *(shin)* leaf is slightly turned to show both its positive and negative sides, with most of the positive side facing the *soe.* The leaves are easily shaped by running them between the moistened thumb and forefinger. When using the Japanese iris for this arrangement the *tai* flower is usually open, while the *shin* flower is always in bud.

In the classical arrangement of the Japanese iris, the emphasis is placed on the leaves. In spring and winter the flowers are arranged shorter than the leaves; in summer and autumn they are taller. In winter it is customary to use only one flower and/or a bud. When a bud and a flower are used, the bud forms part of the *shin* and the flower forms part of the *tai.* If only a bud or a flower is used, it would form part of the tai, and the *shin* would consist of leaves only. A large number of flowers are normally used in early summer. It should also be noted that the *shin* and *tai* leaves are negative leaves and therefore the backs of the leaves should be turned to the viewer, while the *soe* leaves and all leaves to the back of the *shin* are positive leaves and should be placed with their fronts to the viewer. This may be clearly determined by noting that the positive or front of the leaf is concave while the negative or back of the leaf is convex.

This arrangement is a right-hand arrangement. Even in left-hand arrangements, however, the *soe* should always be on the prow side of the boat. The water in the container should not be visible to the viewer lest it suggest a sinking ship to one of a superstitious nature.

Boat arrangements are traditionally always classified as *sô* or cursive, but obviously the arrangement shown here has much of the *shin* or straight quality. The container should rest on a thin, flat base.

An adaptation of this truly classical and simple arrangement may be made in any shallow bowl using a needle-point holder. The needle-point holder should be covered with pebbles to conceal it from view.

FIG. 43. The relative lengths of the leaves and flowers for this boat arrangement are clearly illustrated. The order of arrangement is from left to right.

FIG. 44. The material is held in place by a forked twig.

FIG. 45. Front view, showing leaves and flowers held in place by the *kubari*.

FIG. 46. Side view.

PLATE 20. IRIS ENSATA

In an arrangement of the Iris ensata, the traditional flower for Boy's Day, emphasis is placed on the flowers, of which up to fifteen may be used. The minimum number is two; thereafter only odd numbers are used.

The *shin* is always an open flower and is always taller than the leaves. In an arrangement of only two flowers, the secondary flower may be a supporting flower for the *shin*, or it may be the *soe* or *tai*. It may be either an open flower or a bud.

In this left-hand arrangement of five flowers, the *shin* is two and one-half times the height of the container and is supported by an open flower to the rear and a bud to the front. The *soe* is an open flower and the *tai* a bud. Apart from the *shin* flower, there are no set rules as to whether the flowers should be open or in bud, but for a well balanced arrangement it is preferable to use both. The style of the arrangement is *shin* or straight.

The bronze container known as *shikai-nami* ("waves of the four seas") was introduced by a former head of the Ikenobô School. Inscribed on the front of the container is *"shikai-nami Ikenobô,"* and accordingly its use is confined to the Ikenobô School (see also text to Pl. 23). It stands on a red base known as an *usuban* and a black base called a *kaban*. Either of these bases may be red or black in color; however, the usual combination is red on red or red on black. These bases were originally used by the head of the school, but they are now used by teachers of a certain grade who hold a certificate issued by the head of the school authorizing their use. The *usuban* ranks two grades lower than the *kaban*.

FIG. 47. Relative lengths of the material and order of arrangement from left to right.

PLATE 21. GREAT REED AND THE YELLOW WATER LILY

Gyodô-ike ("fish path,") and *suiriku-ike* ("water and land") are two styles of arrangements which although very similar in style are governed by different rules. They both express coolness and are popular during the summer.

The arrangement illustrated here is the "fish path" —so called because there is a "path" for the fish to swim through. It is arranged in two parts with two different water plants or with one flowering water plant such as the iris or the yellow water lily. One plant forms the *shin* and the *soe,* which are placed to the rear, and the other forms the *tai.* A plant which is common to both land and water, such as the reed, may be used either as a land or a water plant. Unlike the water and land arrangement in which a land plant is separated from a water plant by a dividing stone, in the "fish path"

arrangement a dividing stone is never used.

In this right-hand arrangement the *shin* is twice the length of the container. The *soe* is two-thirds the length of the *shin* and together with the *shin* is placed in the container's left rear quadrant. The tip of the *soe* is in line with a fifty-degree angle drawn from the center of the container to the left rear. The *nejime* of yellow water lilies, which comprises the *tai,* is placed in the container's right front quadrant. The long *tai* leaf is one-third the length of the *shin,* and the right point of the *tai* is in line with a forty-five degree angle drawn from the center of the container to the right front. The *kubari* is usually hidden from view by pebbles. The wormwood container rests on a base of laced bamboo. A low shallow container is always used, and the arrangement is always in the cursive or *sô* style.

Fig. 48. Order of arrangement of the iris from left to right. This arrangement can be made separately (iris without peach blossoms) in a shallow container with a needle-point holder.

PLATE 22. PEACH BLOSSOMS AND JAPANESE IRIS

This is the combination of a land plant and a water plant known as *suiriku-ike,* a water and land arrangement. It is similar in style to the "fish path" arrangement of the preceding plate but differs in that the *shin* and *soe* are usually a land plant and the *tai* is usually a water plant, and the land plant is always placed to the rear of the water plant. Also, a dividing stone is always used. Plants which are common to both land and water, such as the reed, may be used either as a land or a water plant. The rule requiring that the land plant be placed to the rear of the water plant gives an unusual variation in style to this arrangement. For example, the *shin* and *soe* are usually to the rear of the *tai,* but in accordance with this rule, if the water plant is tall (such as the bulrush) and the land plant is short (such as the pink), the tall bulrush becomes *shin* and *soe* and must be placed in front of the short land plant, which becomes *tai.*

In this right-hand arrangement of peach blossoms and Iris laevigata, the *shin* is one and one-half times the length of the container. The placement in the container of the *shin* and *soe* and the *nejime* of iris which comprises the *tai* is the same as for the "fish path" arrangement. The dividing stone is always placed at the base of the land plant and at an angle which makes the whole arrangement form a diagonal across the container. Another rule for this type of arrangement is that the tall *tai* leaf or flower should follow the *shin* curve.

As in the "fish path," the *kubari* is usually concealed from view with pebbles.

The style of arrangement is always cursive or *sô.*

Fig. 49. Side view of the arrangement.

PLATE 23. PINE AND CAMELLIAS

As the camellia flower falls rather quickly, its symbolism in flower arrangement has not always been a happy one, for in feudal times it was usually associated with the samurai whose heads were apt to fall in much the same way. Tradition has it that an arrangement of camellias in the presence of a samurai indicated his time was rather short. However, it is more commonly considered as a flower symbolizing longevity and good fortune. Combinations of camellias with either pine or willow are popular for New Year arrangements.

In this left-hand arrangement, the *shin* is two and one-half times the height of the container and consists of three branches of young pine, one to the front and one to the rear of the *shin*. The *soe* consists of two branches of pine, and the *tai* is made up of the *nejime* of camellias. The order of arrangement is, first the camellias, then the *shin* branches, and finally the two *soe* branches.

The bronze container is the same "waves of the four seas" type as that described under Plate 20. Etiquette requires that its engraved surface be turned away from the viewer when the container holds an arrangement; it is here turned to the front to show the engraving. The style of arrangement is *shin* or straight.

PLATE 24.   PINE AND CHRYSANTHEMUMS

The pine, symbol of longevity, and the chrysanthe-mum, symbol of immortality, are both a happy and popular combination which may be seen at any time throughout the year. The lichen-covered branches indicate a tree of great age and are beautifully used in all phases of Japanese flower arrangement. A feature of the tree plant is that even a single branch can be bent and moulded to suggest the character of the entire tree. The pine is particularly suitable for this.

This single branch of pine has a natural *shin* and *soe* line and required a minimum of rearranging. Being an evergreen, it requires a *nejime* of flowers. In this arrangement, seven chrysanthemums comprise the *tai,* which is the *nejime.*

The order of arrangement of the seven chrysanthe-mums is first the *tai* point, which is the flower inclining to the right shoulder; then, in graded order from tallest to shortest, the three flowers next to the *tai* point; next, the flower in front of the tall *shin* chrys-anthemum; then the *shin* chrysanthemum; and finally the flower to the rear of the *shin* chrysanthemum. The pine branch is placed to the back of the seven chrys-anthemums.

The container is an old earthenware jar known as *kame-tsubo* and stands on a base called a *shiki-dai.* This base would be out of order if the arrangement were to be used on a formal occasion; a plain, black, square base would then be used. This is a right-hand arrange-ment in the *gyô* or semi-cursive style.

FIG. 50. The branches are held in place by four crossed bars known as *izutsu-kubari*. Side view.

PLATE 25. THE TREE PEONY

Classical arrangements are steeped in tradition and bound by stringent rules. The peony, which is considered the king of flowers and the symbol of prosperity, is no exception. Tradition demands that arrangements of peonies consist of only two or three flowers. The *tai* flower should be in full bloom, and the other flowers should be in bud and should not appear below the open flower. The *shin* should be either a dead branch or a young branch in bud with leaves. The *soe* should be of the same material as the *shin*. Leaves should be grouped in levels, of which there may be either two, three, or five. In place of the usual forked twig, four crossed bars in the shape of a well, known as *izutsu-kubari*, are used to hold the material in place. This type of *kubari* is used for the peony and for an arrangement of pine, bamboo, and plum.

In this right-hand arrangement the *shin* and *soe* consist of dead branches. The *shin* is approximately three times the height of the container. The *tai* is an open flower; two buds support the *shin* and *soe* branches. The leaves are arranged in two groups at the lower and middle levels. The peony is always arranged alone.

As here, a base is seldom used under a basket arrangement. The style of arrangement is semi-cursive or *gyô*.

PLATE 26. THE HERBACEOUS PEONY

Unlike the tree peony, the herbaceous peony is not so bound by tradition. This flower may be used alone or with other material, and either flowers and buds or all open flowers may be used.

In this left-hand arrangement of nine flowers, the *shin* is two and one-half times the height of the basket. If open flowers and buds are used, the *shin* and *soe* may be buds, but the *tai* is usually an open flower. Flowers are usually arranged in odd numbers from .three to fifteen; there is also an arrangement of two flowers.

The style of arrangement is semi-cursive or *gyô*.

FIG. 51. The relative lengths of the flowers are clearly illustrated. Order of arrangement is from left to right. The *tai* is the first flower and *soe* the last flower to be arranged. From the left, the first three flowers are *tai* flowers, the next four *shin* flowers, and the last two *soe* flowers.

FIG. 52. The stems are held firmly in place by the *kubari*. All the stems should rest firmly on the base of the container. Side view.

Shôka Arrangements   85

Fig. 53. As with other material, the leaves are held firmly in place by a forked twig. Side view.

PLATE 27. THE YELLOW DAY LILY

The day lily is usually arranged alone and should consist of only two flowers: an open flower for the *shin* branch and a bud to support the *tai* leaves.

In this right-hand arrangement the *shin* is twice the height of the container. The *tai* bud is approximately half the height of the *shin*. The *tai* leaves, which hang down to the right front, should consist of old and new leaves and in this arrangement they support the bud, which faces the *shin*. The *soe* leaf on the left of the arrangement is an old one. The tall leaves which appear to the center support the *shin* and are new ones. In this form of arrangement, the placement of the old and new leaves is important, and the *shin* line should be kept as free as possible.

The style of arrangement is *gyô* or semi-cursive.

Although it has been stated that baskets are seldom used with a base, in this case laced bamboo has been used. Many baskets have built-in legs or bases, and in such cases a separate base is not used. In this arrangement the basket is flat-bottomed and accordingly a thin base is permissible.

PLATE 28. THE HOSTA

The hosta (also called funkia or plantain lily) and the aster, both popular in classical arrangements, are classified as "leaf plants" and are arranged primarily for the beauty of their leaves. Usually two or three flowers are used with odd numbers of leaves. The popular choice is two flowers with three, five, or seven leaves. When two flowers are used, one may be the *shin* and the other the *tai,* or both may be the *shin.* This is decided by the number of leaves used. The *shin* flower is twice the height of the level of the highest leaf.

In this right-hand arrangement of three leaves and two flowers, the height of the *shin* flower is twice the width of the container and twice the height of the level of the highest leaf, which in this arrangement is the *soe.* This differs from the usual form of arrangement in which the *soe* is two-thirds the height of the *shin.* The *tai* is one-third the height of the *shin.* The *tai* leaf is turned down to show both positive and negative sides; the *shin* leaf shows only its negative side; the *soe* leaf shows both positive and negative sides. A needle-point holder, hidden from view by pebbles, holds the material in place. Order of arrangement is, first, the *tai* leaf, followed by the *shin* leaf, two *shin* flowers, and, finally, the *soe* leaf.

This style of arrangement is known as *gyaku-zoe,* or inverted *soe,* and differs from the usual form of arrangement in that the *soe* leaf does not follow the *shin* curve. ·This means that the positions of the *soe* and *tai* in relation to the *shin* have been reversed; however, the positive side of the arrangement remains unchanged. From the position of the viewer, the front of the *shin,* which in this arrangement is the right-hand side of the arrangement, is the positive side. The hosta and the aster are usually arranged alone.

The style of arrangement is cursive or *sô.*

FIG. 54. The numbers indicate the order of arrangement. For a left-hand arrangement the entire arrangement would be reversed.

FIG. 55. The placement of the leaves and flowers in the needle-point holder can be easily accomplished by following the numbers. For a left-hand arrangement leaves 3 and 4 are reversed; likewise leaves 6 and 7.

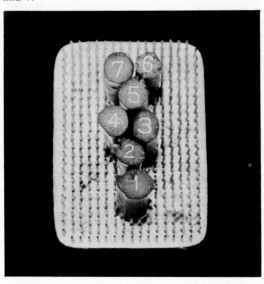

PLATE 29. THE ARUM LILY

The arum or calla lily also is classified as a "leaf plant" and accordingly is arranged primariiy for the beauty of its leaves. An arrangement usually consists of two or three flowers with odd numbers of leaves. A popular arrangement is two flowers with five leaves.

In this right-hand arrangement, the *shin* consists of one lily and two leaves, the *tai* of one lily and two leaves, and the *soe* of one leaf. If a comparison is made with the previous plate, it will be noted that when the minimum number of three leaves is used, the *shin* consists of two flowers and one leaf, and the *soe* and *tai* of one leaf each.

The tall *shin* lily is approximately one and a half times the width of the container. The *soe* leaf is two-thirds the height of the *shin*, and the *tai* leaf is one-third the height of the *shin*. The *tai* lily is a little more than one-half the height of the *shin* lily. The *tai* (1) is placed in the holder with its back to the viewer and at an angle of 45° toward the right shoulder. Next follows the *tai* lily (2), which stands rather erect. The other *tai* leaf (3) is placed slightly to the right rear facing the *tai* lily. The leaf to the front of the *shin* (4) is placed with its back to the viewer and facing the *shin* lily. The *shin* (5) stands erect with its flower directly in line with the base of its stem. The leaf to the back of the *shin* (6) inclines to the rear and faces the *shin* lily. The *soe* leaf (7) is placed at an angle of 45° to the left rear. A vertical line dropped from the *shin* flower to its base should touch the tip of the leaf to the back of the *shin* (6) and the inner side of the *tai* flower (2). In this arrangement the *tai* lily is facing the *shin;* however, the *tai* lily may also face in the same direction as the *shin* lily. Either way is in order.

A needle-point holder, concealed from view by pebbles, has here been used to hold the leaves and flowers. It is also wise when doing this arrangement to tie the ends of the stems with raffia or some other such flexible material to prevent them from splaying. Finally, a sliver of bamboo or any other suitable material inserted into the stems of the flowers and leaves will assist in holding them firmly in position.

A low, wide-mouthed, shallow container of ceramic ware is preferred. The arrangement is in the *sô* or cursive style.

FIG. 56. Back view of the gourd-shaped basket and bamboo inner container. The board has a sliding screw attached to the slot. In classical Ikenobô this board is usually plain with a fixed peg and no slot.

FIG. 57. Although the container is quite narrow, a forked twig is used to hold the branches in place. Side view.

PLATE 30. THE CLEMATIS

Wall arrangements fall into two categories: arrangements which hang on the wall and are viewed from the front *(mukô-gake)*, and arrangements which hang on a pillar to be viewed from the side *(yokô-gake)*.

Either one or two kinds of materials may be used. If two kinds are used, the *shin* and *soe* should be the same and the *tai* should be different material. The method of arrangement is the same as for the upper level of the *nijû-ike* of Plate 12. The *shin* is always the longest branch and when hanging may measure up to three times the height of the container. In either a wall or side arrangement, all three branches should not hang down, and in a wall arrangement the *tai* should not extend beyond the outer edge of the container.

In this wall arrangement, the hanging branch is the *shin,* and its length is about twice the height of the container. The tall flower is *soe* and the short one is *tai.* This is a left-hand arrangement.

The container is a gourd-shaped basket hanging on a board known as a *suibachi.* Wall arrangements are always in the *sô* or cursive form.

PLATE 31. THE SEVEN GRASSES OF AUTUMN

The seven grasses of autumn, immortalized in a poem written by Okura Yamanoue (660–733), are popular in all schools of Japanese flower arrangement. Consisting of the pink, Chinese bellflower, thoroughwort, patrinia, miscanthus, bush clover, and the kudzu vine, they comprise the only classical *shôka* arrangement in which more than three kinds of materials are used.

In this right-hand arrangement the length of the *shin,* which is the tall miscanthus, is approximately three times the width of the container. The *shin* consists of miscanthus, patrinia, and bush clover. The *soe* is comprised of the bush clover and the kudzu vine; the *tai* is made up of the pink, Chinese bellflower, thoroughwort, and one leaf of the kudzu vine.

Order of placement in the forked twig or *kubari* is, first, the pink and the kudzu leaf, followed by the bellflowers and thoroughwort. Next follow the patrinia and miscanthus, with the bush clover being placed to the right rear behind the miscanthus. Bush clover is also then placed to the left to support the *soe* branch of kudzu vine, which trails to the left and is the last branch to be placed in position.

The container is known as a *Fuji-kago,* a basket shaped like Mount Fuji. The style of arrangement is *gyô* or semi-cursive.

Fig. 58. The numbers indicate the sequence in which the leaves and berries are arranged.

Plate 32. The Rhodea Japonica

The Japanese name for this plant is *omoto,* written with characters meaning "green for ten thousand years." The leaves symbolize maturity, and the berries, the fruits of life. Since the plant itself is symbolic of eternal youth, this is quite a popular arrangement on felicitous occasions, being particularly favored for weddings.

Unlike the other classical arrangements, which are all based on the *shin, soe,* and *tai,* an arrangement of this plant, which grows four new leaves a year, is based on four principal leaves, namely, the standing leaf *(tachiba),* the leaf receiving dew *(tsuyu-ukeba),* the front leaf *(maeba),* and the long leaf *(nagashiba).* Three of these leaves may be reconciled with a *shin, soe, tai* arrangement: *tachiba* as the *shin, tsuyu-ukeba* as the *soe,* and *maeba* as the *tai.* The measurements for these leaves are the same as for the *shin, soe,* and *tai.* The fourth leaf is the long *nagashiba,* an extra leaf which is slightly shorter than the *tachiba.* The leaves are always arranged in even numbers from six to twelve with one cluster of berries.

In this left-hand arrangement of twelve leaves as numbered in Fig. 58, the *shin* leaf *(tachiba,* No. 1) is a little more than one and one-half times the width of the container and is placed with its back or negative side to the viewer. It is supported by leaves 3 and 4. The *soe* leaf *(tsuyu-ukeba,* No. 2) is placed to the right rear with its front or positive side facing the *tachiba.* It is supported by leaf 12. The *tai* leaf *(maeba,* No. 11) is placed in the front of the arrangement with the tip of the leaf slightly to the left and turned down to show both the positive and negative sides. It is supported by leaves 8–10. The additional leaf *(nagashiba,* No. 6) trails out to the left and is supported by leaf 7. The berries (No. 5) are placed in the center, and leaf 13 is a supporting leaf for the whole arrangement.

The rhodea is usually arranged in a low, shallow container. This is a *sô* or cursive arrangement.

PLATE 33.   PLUM

The plum (actually Japanese flowering apricot, Prunus Mume), symbol of longevity, expresses many virtues such as innocence, nobleness, and courage. It is used on felicitous occasions particularly during the New Year festivities.

This left-hand arrangement of early plum blossoms illustrates the natural *shin* and *soe* lines to be found in a single branch. It also shows the natural beauty of line of a branch free of foliage.

The *shin* and *soe* consist of one branch of material. The *shin* is approximately three times the height of the container, the *soe* two-thirds the length of the *shin*. The *tai* is approximately one-third the length of the *shin*.

The arrangement is held in place by a forked twig, and stands in a bronze container known as an *ogencho,* which resembles the small round wooden table termed *maru-sambô* used for altar offerings. It is engraved with the characters "*ogencho* Ikenobô" and was introduced by the Ikenobô master Senmyô XLI. As previously explained, etiquette requires that, when the container is used for an arrangement, the engraved portion be turned away from the viewer. The style of arrangement is *gyô* or semi-cursive.

PLATE 34. PINE, BAMBOO, AND PLUM

An arrangement of pine, bamboo, and plum (Prunus Mume) is the most popular arrangement for a felicitous occasion. Symbolic of longevity, these materials are widely used during the New Year season. The arrangement may be made by combining the three materials in one container, or each one in a separate container. If three containers are used, the pine should be placed in the center with the bamboo on the viewer's right and the plum on the left. A *nejime* of seasonal flowers should be arranged with the pine and the bamboo.

In this right-hand arrangement the *shin* and *soe* are plum, and the *tai* is pine, while a tall branch of bamboo supports the *shin*. The length of the *shin* is a little more than three times the height of the container. The *soe,* normally two-thirds the length of the *shin,* is approximately half the length of the *shin;* this is because of the tall bamboo supporting the *shin*. If the *soe* were its normal length, the arrangement would be top-heavy. The *tai* is approximately one-third the length of the *shin*.

The bamboo is the most important element in this type of arrangement, and requires special attention.

First, it should always be placed to the front of the arrangement. This gives it precedence over the *tai,* which is usually placed to the front of the arrangement. The number of nodes on the main branch should be an odd number, with the lowest node appearing approximately one inch above the water-level. Finally, the top of the branch should be cut perfectly straight, never on the slant.

There are no set rules governing the use of materials for the three branches, but the following combinations are most common: (a) The *shin* of young pine supported by bamboo; the *soe* and *tai* of plum. (b) The *shin* and *soe* of plum, with the former supported by bamboo; the *tai* of pine. (c) The *shin* and *soe* of pine, with the former supported by plum; the *tai* of bamboo leaves. (d) The *shin* and *soe* of plum, with the former supported by pine; the *tai* of bamboo leaves.

The branches are held in place by the four-crossbar *izutsu-kubari*. This type of *kubari* is used for this arrangement, and for an arrangement of the tree peony.

The arrangement stands in a large bronze *usubata* on a black base *(kaban)*. The style of arrangement is *gyô* or semi-cursive.

PLATE 35. KALE, PUSSY WILLOW, AND DRIFTWOOD

Although Ikenobô, like other schools of Japanese flower arrangement, has its modern branch, this arrangement is not an example of the modern school of Ikenobô, but rather a contemporary arrangement in the classical style. Although no container has been used and the material has been combined with driftwood, it still has a strong classical feeling.

The seventeen branches of pussy willow comprise the *shin* and *soe* branches. One piece of driftwood supports the *shin* and the other piece supports the *soe*. The *nejime* of five small variegated kale, which are widely used throughout Japan during the New Year season, comprise the *tai*. The two short branches of pussy willow to the rear of the arrangement are termed *tai-oku* ("in from *tai*"); they are the last branches to be added to the arrangement.

This is a right-hand arrangement in the cursive or *sô* style.

Part Two

Modern Arrangements

~ 6 ~ Introduction

"AN ART of flower arrangement which is often done without the use of flowers and which makes use of tree stumps, roots, wires, branches which are worked into shape or left as formed, and bits of cement—in brief, an art which excludes no material as long as it is of use in form, color, or power of suggestion; an art which ranges from a single flower or a bare branch placed in a vase to a monumental construction which decorates a garden, a public place, or a square in the realm of city-planning: therein lie the qualities which astonish those fearful of departing from the treaded path and who are constantly lagging behind." The foregoing, extracted from a commentary by Alfred Smoular on an exhibition by Sôfû Teshigahara, seems a fitting introduction to the second part of this book—a part devoted to the new in Japanese flower arrangement.

From the time of the introduction, early in this century, of the *moribana* style, a style which allowed considerable latitude in the choice and disposition of materials, there has been a steady development toward complete freedom of expression in flower arrangement. As related in the historical section of this volume, the final break with all traditional ties was expressed by a group of flower masters and critics in 1930. Impeded by the war, this movement spread rapidly in the early postwar years, and today the modern schools of flower arrangement are predominant. In reviewing the history of this art, it is of interest to note that what appear to be some of the most active periods in its development are those following long periods of civil strife or war. As though seeking outlets of tranquillity and beauty, there has been a return by the masses to this age-old art which has considerably enhanced both its development and popularity.

This modern interpretation utilizes all forms of plant life, living or dead in every conceivable form—whole tree trunks, stumps, roots, grasses, flowers, vines; all varieties of dried material (grasses, flowers, trees, roots, vines, seaweed) either in natural colors or sprayed or painted. It may be used with or without a container. The container may be of the conventional type or may be one of the arranger's invention such as automotive parts or drain-piping. It may be used alone or in conjunction with other non-floral material such as wrought iron, scrap metal, wire, stone, brass, vinyl, feathers, glass, foam glass, sponges, seaweed, sea shells. This non-vegetable material may even form the primary element of the arrangement. The arrangements may also be created in mobile form or in the form of a wall relief set in plaster of Paris. This broadness of interpretation has been expanded to the point where non-floral material such as wrought iron, stone, etc., may be used alone. These non-floral "things," whether alone or in conjunction with floral material, are now commonly referred to as *objets,* a term which now forms part of the Japanese vocabulary.

This free expression now so widely interpreted by the numerous schools is in some of its more extreme forms a little startling to the un-initiated. To the student, however, this is not so, for he is well acquaint-ed with its motivating force—design. As has been expressed by others, it is not what is put together but how it is put together. A great num-ber of the masters, particularly those who head the various schools, have grown up with the art from their earliest years. Whether it was classical or free style, it recognized a basic design. Their long associa-tion with an art although limited in form developed the ability to dis-cern and utilize design in plant life, and made them perfectionists in their field. It was natural, therefore, that along with an increasing freedom in the selection and placement of materials, there should be a development toward creative expression. Now completely unfettered, modern Japanese flower arrangement is infinite in its creativeness. As expressed by Alfred Smoular in his commentary on the master Sôfû Teshigahara, this expansion into fields seemingly outside the realm of floral art "has not reduced the role of wild flowers or cultivated flowers but has rather expanded it. He has expanded the botanical domain by creating new species, combining clashing forms and colors, and giving to inert bodies without any perfume certain attributes which had hither-to only been accorded to flowers."

Just as the *rikka* form was the popular choice of the nobility and samurai three centuries ago, so is this new style of arrangement based on free expression the popular choice of today. Flower arrangement, like other living arts, is influenced by the age in which we live and ex-presses the mood of contemporary life. Its great popularity is due to the ability of the masters to adapt it to present-day conditions and to their creative ability in expanding the art by introducing new forms both in materials and ideas.

The arrangements forming the second part of this book are presented in two parts—Free-Style Arrangements and Basic Lessons—and are based on the Sôgetsu School, the foremost of the schools devoted en-tirely to free expression. Founded in 1926 by Sôfû Teshigahara, this school in the short space of thirty-odd years has grown to be one of the largest in Japan. Under the leadership of Sôfû Teshigahara, a man of untiring and infinite creative capacity who has successfully adapted his art to all phases of present-day activity, it plays a leading role in the field of Japanese flower arrangement.

For the student, complete mastery of the lessons is a basic requirement. Not only will a full knowledge of these styles enable the arranger to make many beautiful arrangements, but their mastery will lead to free-style arrangements based on the arranger's own creative ability. Taking form, line, space, texture, and color harmony as his basis, all of which form part of the basic lessons, the student should strive to be creative and original. He should absorb and copy only to the extent of mastering the lessons. The idea for an arrangement should come from the material to be used or the container which is to hold the arrangement or from a preconceived design. Above all, the arrangement should be endowed with feeling. The material should be carefully studied and utilized to its best advantage to express the feelings of the arranger.

In creating an arrangement a title may be given to express the feelings of the arranger. Rarely are exhibition pieces created by the masters unnamed.

It will be noted that, whereas a wooden base of some form is used with practically all classical arrangements, no such bases are used with modern arrangements. A base may be used only if it enhances the arrangement, and this is seldom the case with modern arrangements. When no container is used, the arrangement usually stands on coarse sand or crushed rock sometimes sprayed a suitable color. It is also important to note that accessories are not used.

It seems appropriate to mention briefly something of the containers used in the free-style arrangements in this volume. Forming part of the author's collection, they are considered fairly representative of the work performed by present-day Japanese potters for flower arrangement. The author will feel he has failed in his purpose if they only evoke such a comment as "But where can I obtain a container like that?" It is the intention here to present Japanese flower arrangement as it is practiced in Japan today. In a land where flower arranging is engaged in on a large scale, demand has created a vast and attractive supply of containers. Should the student be limited in his own supply, many beautiful arrangements can be made with the basic *moribana* and *nageire* containers illustrated in the basic lessons. It is better still if the student is prompted to improvise and utilize the many attractive and often discarded articles which may be found lying idle in the average home in any country (bottles, lids, pitchers, baskets, ash trays, and so forth). Whatever is used, it should form an integral part of the whole design.

~ 7 ~ Free-style Arrangements : Plates 36-85

IN THE first part of this book, concerning classical arrangements, the chronological order was followed, with *rikka* treated first and then *shôka*, since the beginnings of the three-branch asymmetrical *shôka* form are clearly seen in the *rikka* form from which it developed. In turning to modern arrangements, however, it has been thought best to deal first, in this chapter, with the present popular free style and then, in the following chapter of basic lessons, to go back a bit in time to the *moribana* and *nageire* styles. For one thing, the connection between the latter styles and free-style arrangements is not as readily apparent as that between *rikka* and *shôka*. And, secondly, these free-style arrangements deserve special emphasis in that they are in a sense the epitome of the modern flower arrangement as contrasted with the classical.

While the following free-style arrangements are considered representative of the work one may see in Japan in the home, studio, and exhibition hall today, it should be kept in mind that they are the work of but a single man and therefore limited. The work of one person necessarily differs from that of another. Also, in a school of free expression it is inevitable that one will develop one's own style. It is hoped, then, that these arrangements will serve as a basis for further study and thus contribute to better flower arrangement.

PLATE 36. A modern *nageire* arrangement of Japanese flowering quince and camellias by Sôfû Teshigahara, founder and head of the Sôgetsu School.

Nageire, one of the oldest styles of Japanese floral art, originally consisted of only two branches or flowers, which symbolized the positive and negative aspects of Oriental philosophy. Also, as in the classical arrangements illustrated earlier in this volume, the stems were free of any foliage for a height of several inches from the mouth of the container. In modern *nageire,* however, there is complete freedom of choice in the selection of containers and materials, and the foliage or flowers lightly cover the mouth of the container.

◀ PLATE 37. This striking black and white container by K. Yasuhara of Tokyo is emphasized by a simple arrangement of one anthurium leaf and torch ginger. The unnatural but interesting shape of the stem made it possible for the leaf to be placed above the flower as though suspended in air.

▲

PLATE 38. One learns to be merciless with flowers in the study of this fascinating art in Japan. Here, for example, the heads of three strelitzia have been cut off and massed low to blend in with the three points of the unusual wrought-iron container.

Free-Style Arrangements 109

PLATE 39. Heavily lichen-covered branches of Japanese quince massed around a single head of torch ginger in a large black bowl form this grotesque but interesting pattern.

PLATE 41. Three dried sunflowers, an austere branch of distylium, and the unglazed container combine to form this monochrome arrangement which highlights the natural beauty of the sunflowers.

PLATE 42. A miniature arrangement of Australian native rose, five inches high. Miniature arrangements in containers as small as thimbles form a part of contemporary Japanese flower arrangement.

PLATE 43. The camellia, one of the most com- ▶ monly used flowers in Japanese floral art, is arranged here at the base of a branch of fasciated willow. The curve of the willow follows the curve of the container. The arrangement stands by a sunlit Japanese window.

PLATE 44. Four small striped-glass containers have been placed one upon the other to provide the setting for a single head of red ginger and two dried branches of edgeworthia which have been stripped of their bark and painted black. This material, known in Japan as *mitsumata* because of its three-pronged branches, is widely used in modern arrangements. Its long, straight lines lend themselves admirably to modern design. Whether used simply or in large quantities, it offers infinite possibilities.

PLATE 45. Dried gleditsia pods painted a dull black and combined with two sunflowers in a two-level yellow-and-black lacquer container designed by Sôfû Teshigahara. The container, a modern version of the classical two-level bamboo container, can be dismantled and used in numerous different patterns.

PLATE 46. Two cattleyas rest on three glass objects which have been arranged to give the effect of broken ice. Glass by T. Iwata of Tokyo.

Plate 47. Dried grass and a withered monstera leaf sprayed black have been combined to blend with the color of this modern unglazed-pottery container.

PLATE 48. A dry arrangement of Australian everlasting daisies and dried aspidistra leaves in a partially glazed container by Suzuki of Kyoto. Japan abounds with beautiful aspidistra leaves, which are a basic necessity for classical arrangements. They have been effectively incorporated into modern arrangements in their natural or dried state, or by spraying them with various colors while they are still green.

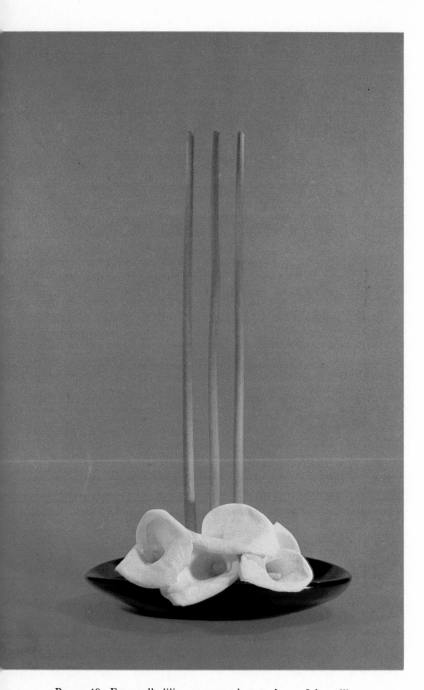

PLATE 49. Four calla lilies are massed at the base of three lily
stems. Care has been taken in the placement of the lilies, no
two of which face in the same direction. Slivers of bamboo
inserted through the stems hold them upright.

PLATE 50. A line arrangement of dried foxtails and grass with one chrysanthemum. Container by the author.

PLATE 51. Water lilies are widely seen throughout Japan during the summer months. This arrangement of four lilies and a bud in a large black bowl expresses a feeling of coolness.

PLATE 52. The traditional combination of pine and camellias provides an attractive table arrangement with one branch of lichen-covered pine and a single flower on a red-lacquer plate.

PLATE 53. A mass of trailing spiraea cascades over a cluster of clivia and driftwood. The driftwood has been arranged through the top of the tall black container, which has openings on two sides. The arrangement is approximately five feet high.

PLATE 54. Branches of the hardy orange painted black are combined with Easter lilies for this black and white arrangement. Thorns, never used in classical arrangements, are widely used in contemporary schools.

PLATE 55. Gerberas and part of a dried banana leaf provide a contrast in texture and a harmony of color which blend with the dry feeling of the container. The mass of feathery gerberas does not clutter the mouth of the container and provides an intricate pattern and color against the dried leaf. The two tall flowers balance the arrangement and offset the heaviness of the mass.

PLATE 57. Three Australian waratahs in a peaked glass bowl.

PLATE 58. Lichen-covered branches of Japanese quince are massed with branches of Ilex serrata and tangerines to form this modern *nageire* arrangement. Container by K. Yasuhara of Tokyo. The arrangement is five feet high.

PLATE 59. Burnet stripped of all its leaves gives a
lace-like effect around pampas grass, both blending
with the modern container by Suzuki of Kyoto.

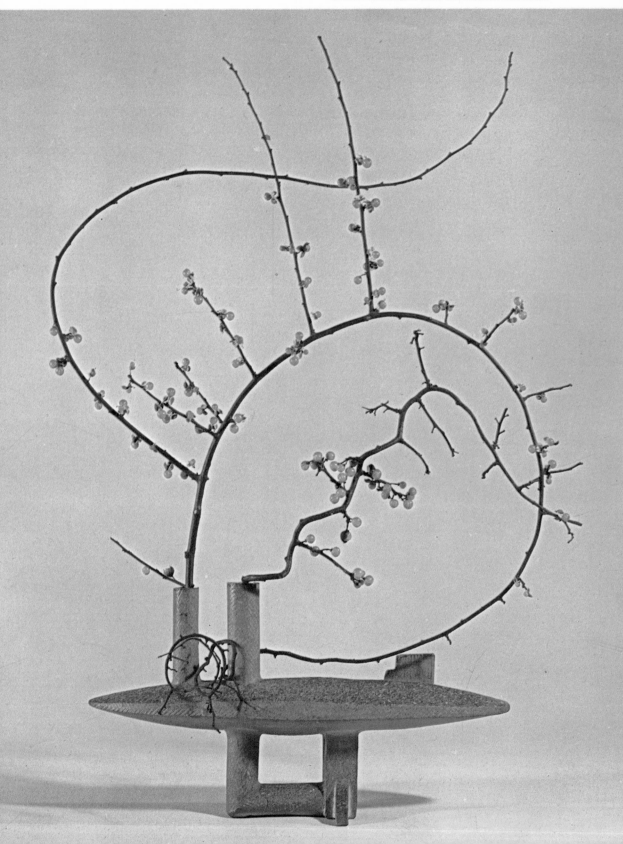

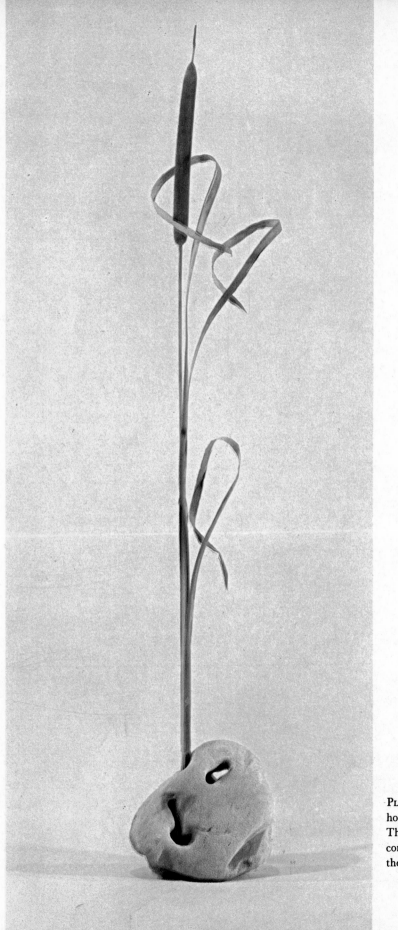

PLATE 61. A natural stone is used as the holder for a cat-tail and its dried leaves. The material in its natural state has been combined into a design which expresses the simplicity of nature.

PLATE 62. Crossed cat-tails and their dried leaves have been arranged to dramatize this modern container. In an arrangement of this kind the container is the focal point of the arrangement.

Free-Style Arrangements 129

PLATE 63. A modern *moribana* arrangement of camellias and Japanese flowering quince. The two branches at the lower left and lower right project forward. Similarly, the camellia at the base projects slightly forward. These projections emphasize the arrangement's three-dimensional effect.

PLATE 65. A single Australian waratah forms the
focal point for this arrangement, in which thick
branches of edgeworthia painted black duplicate the
lines of the container.

PLATE 66. Ginger lilies and edgeworthia painted black in a black and white container designed by Sôfù Teshigahara. The edgeworthia has been cut to duplicate the design of the container.

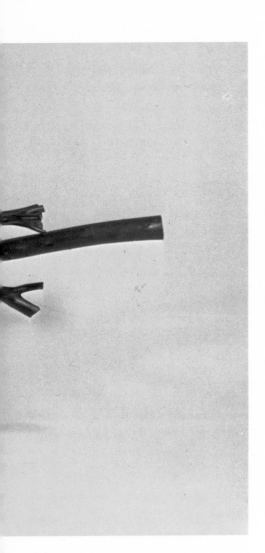

PLATE 67. A simple arrangement of two chrysanthemums and two branches of leucothoe. This type of container lends itself very well to either a low and massed or a tall arrangement.

PLATE 68. The yellow, black, and red lacquer container designed by Sôfû Teshigahara provides the motif for this arrangement. The yellow and black of the container is repeated in the long stems of fuller's teazel, which have been painted yellow and black. The red dot of the container is duplicated by the red capsicum.

134   *Modern Arrangements*

PLATE 69. Thorns of the
hardy orange form the background for a mass of variegated capsicum in a variegated glass bowl.

PLATE 70. This unglazed pipe container provides an effective background for the intricate pattern formed by the bursting seed pods of the red sandalwood tree, which have been displayed to full advantage by arranging them on a vertical plane.

PLATE 71. "COCKTAILS." This gay and carefree arrangement is a combination of bleached palm leaves, dried branches of inula sprayed black, and Australian native rose.

PLATE 72. "RESISTANCE." A single tulip and two
amaryllis leaves simply arranged in an interesting container by K. Ōtsuki of Kyoto.

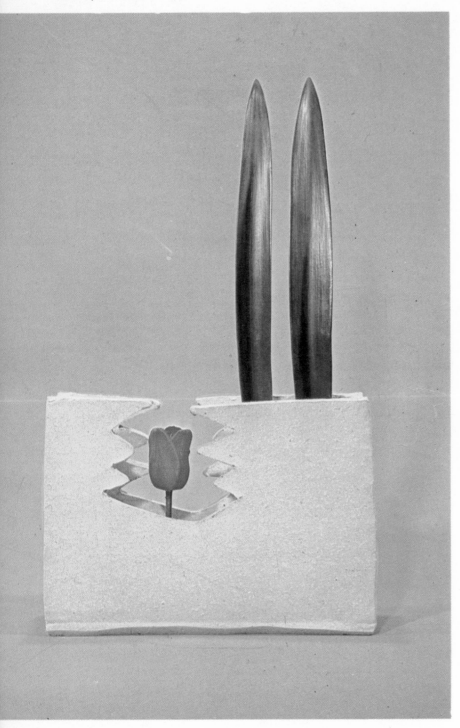

PLATE 73. "BOOMERANGS." The Australian aboriginal weapon is the theme for this arrangement, which was an award-winner in the Tokyo Annual Ikebana Art Exhibition. Cut from sheet iron into various sizes and welded together, the boomerangs have been laced with natural and red edgeworthia. The arrangement is four feet high.

PLATE 74. "STARS." An exhibition piece of wrought iron. Welded together to form an interesting design, the arrangement is viewable from any angle. Despite the absence of flowers, this form of arrangement is accepted at Japanese exhibitions. Suffice it to say that the motivating force for the design is flowers. The arrangement is five feet high.

PLATE 75. "MODESTY." This arrangement features a cluster of red dahlias behind a dried branch of summer cypress which has been painted black. The interesting container is by K. Yasuhara of Tokyo.

PLATE 76. "STUMPS." Five roots provide the design for this exhibition piece. The roots are used in their natural color, and are massed with balls of asparagus fern which have been sprayed green. The arrangement is six feet high.

PLATE 77. "Torso." Limbs of the white birch have been arranged together to form a geometrical pattern. In this style of arrangement the cut surfaces of the limbs play an important part in the design. The height of this exhibition piece is five feet.

142 *Modern Arrangements*

PLATE 78. "THE BLACK SUN." The title of this arrangement is clearly inspired by the dried sunflower painted black, with the brilliant mass of clivia at its base. The container is by Matsushima of Chiba.

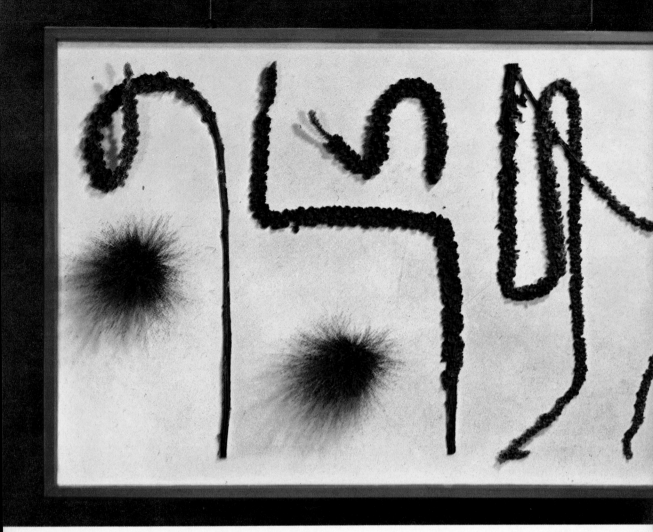

PLATE 79. "CAMEL." A wall relief of dried liatris stalks and two clusters of dried grass set in plaster of Paris in a Chinese-red frame. Its size is three feet by two feet. Plaster of Paris is widely used in modern arrangements. It can be effecively used for covering branches or roots, making interesting objects by covering stones, and making temporary containers by first moulding the base with chicken wire or clay.

PLATE 80. "SPACEMAN." A one-flower arrangement featuring a single cattleya set in stone. Height of arrangement: four feet. Although this has been cut from hard stone, pumice stone, which can be easily cut into various interesting shapes, is widely used.

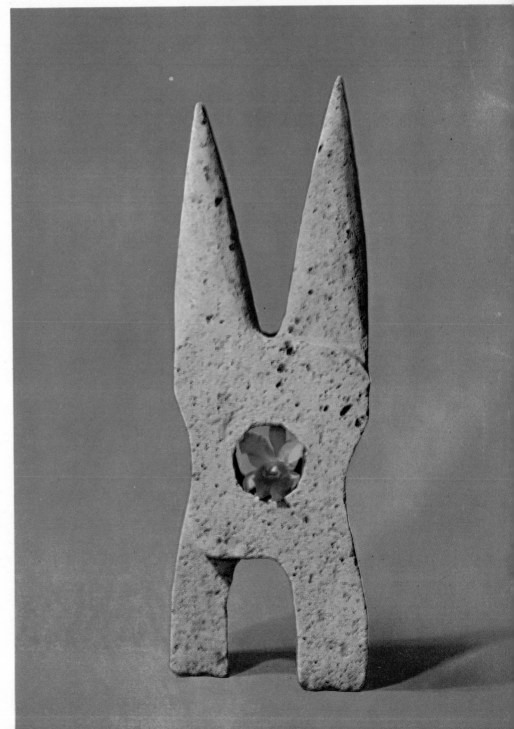

◄ Plate 81. "Mantis." A composition of dried sun-flowers and celastrus arranged in a modern container by Kumamoto of Kyoto.

Plate 82. "Pipes." An exhibition arrangement of seven pieces of bamboo which have been sprayed dark brown. Height of arrangement: four feet.

PLATE 83. An interesting mobile of ceramics and brass pieces suspended by
catgut to float in space. The container at the left is arranged with seed pods of
the red sandalwood tree, and the two on the right with massed celosia and
dried rape stalks. Mobiles of all kinds of material, both floral and metallic, are
widely used in contemporary Japanese flower arrangements.

PLATE 84. "SCHOOL DAYS." Two amaryllis and an artichoke in an unglazed pottery container by K. Ôtsuki of Kyoto.

PLATE 85. "WINTER DANCE." An exhibition piece of wisteria vine and criss-crossed edgeworthia. This arrangement was created for the One-hundred-man Exhibition held annually in Tokyo and Osaka. Height of arrangement: seven feet.

THE FIFTEEN lessons presented here in pictorial form should be carefully studied and their basic principles mastered. Not only will such mastery enable the student to have knowledge of a number of beautiful arrangements but, as previously stated, this knowledge will lead the arranger to develop his own creative ability—for the lessons are but the foundation on which the greater structure of creativity and free expression rests.

The lessons are based on two fundamental styles, *moribana* and *nageire*. *Moribana* is a compound formation from the verb *moru* "to heap up," and the noun *hana* "flower(s)," and hence means "heaped-up flowers." This style of arrangement features a low, shallow container (Fig. 59) in which the material is held in place by a needle-point holder termed *kenzan*. *Nageire* is derived from the verb *nage-ireru,* meaning "to throw (fling) into," and features a tall container (Fig. 60) in which the material rests against the lip of the container, or is held in place by various artifices which will be dealt with as the occasion arises. In this style of arrangement a needle-point holder is not used.

In both the *moribana* and *nageire* styles, the arrangement is based on the asymmetrical placement of three principal branches—the *shin* (primary branch), the *soe* (secondary branch), and the *hikae* (tertiary branch). All supporting branches are termed *jûshi,* this being the counterpart of the classical *ashirai*. The length of these three branches is determined by the type of plant material, the container, and the location of the completed arrangement. The *shin* may be from one to two times the container's length, plus its height. For tall containers, the *shin* may be from one to two times the container's height, plus its diameter. In an average arrangement the *shin* is one and one-half times the container's length or height, plus the container's height or diameter. The *soe* is three-quarters the length of the *shin,* and the *hikae* is three-quarters the length of the *soe*. In large arrangements the *hikae* may be half the length of the *soe*.

While these measurements are sound proportions for any student to follow, they are only approximate, and when the lessons have been mastered the arranger may at times rely on his own judgment.

Unlike classical arrangements there are no restrictions in the use or combination of plant life. This is governed by color harmony, texture, and good taste. However, the beginner would be wise to show restraint and limit himself either to one or two kinds of flowers or to a combination of one kind of foliage and one kind of flower. Although there are no restrictions, combinations of more than three varieties of material

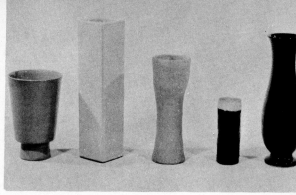

FIG. 59. Typical shallow containers used for *moribana* arrangements.

FIG. 60. Types of tall containers used for *nageire* arrangements.

are rarely used. Non-flowering material such as the pine or willow is seldom used alone; however, tree material which bears blossoms, such as the Japanese quince, is often used alone.

When two kinds of material are used it is common practice for the tertiary branch *(hikae)* to be of different material from the primary and secondary branches *(shin* and *soe)*.

The following are important basic features of good modern arrangements:

1. The needle-point holder used in *moribana* arrangements should never be visible. If the holder slips, place a piece of paper under it. A holder in a transparent glass container may be more easily hidden from view by wrapping it in a piece of white tissue paper.

2. In both *moribana* and *nageire,* the mouth of the container should not be cluttered. The lip of the container should be just lightly covered with foliage or flowers.

3. Special attention should be given to the focal point, which is usually the base of the arrangement; for it is to this part that the viewer's attention is first drawn. It is preferable to use flowers in this part of the arrangement.

4. Generally speaking, when arranging a single type of flower characterized more by the color of its blossom than by its beauty of line, thick masses should be avoided. Utilize space by creating space between the flowers or stems. However, when it is necessary to use a cluster of flowers at the base of an arrangement, the flowers in this portion should be massed densely. For good color effect, remove all foliage.

5. Think of the arrangement as a whole and not of the beauty of the individual flowers. Arrange the flowers facing each other rather than all facing the viewer. A knowledge of the positive and negative principles, referred to in Chapter 1, is likewise valuable here.

6. Study the plant material carefully before placing it in the container. Select the best branch or flower for the *shin* and dispose the other material as though the *shin* were the sun.

7. With "tree material," study the branch carefully to discern the latent beauty of line through the foliage. Do not hesitate to bring out this beauty by cutting away all unnecessary branches or flowers.

8. Utilize space by eliminating all unnecessary material and by the judicious placement of the material.

9. Endow the arrangement with feeling. Allow it to express your own mood.

10. Remember the basic design.

LESSON 1. MORIBANA. BASIC UPRIGHT STYLE.

Material: five chrysanthemums

1. FIG. 61. The *shin* or primary branch is approximately twice the width, plus the height, of the container. The *soe* or secondary branch is three-quarters the length of the *shin*. The *hikae* or tertiary branch is three-quarters the length of the *soe*. The remaining two flowers are termed *jūshi,* the supporting flowers or branches. While there are no set rules for the length or number of *jūshi,* they should not be longer than any one of the three main branches which they support. In this lesson they support the *hikae,* which is the shortest of the three main branches, and accordingly are shorter than the *hikae.*

FIG. 65

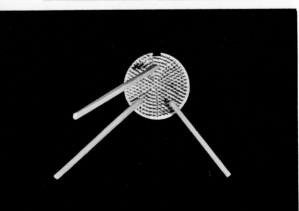

2.   FIG. 62.   The needle-point holder is placed in the left front of the container. The *shin* is placed at an angle of 15° toward the left shoulder.

3.   FIG. 63.   The *soe* is placed at an angle of 45° toward the left shoulder, just a little to the left of the *shin*.

4.   FIG. 64.   The *hikae* is placed at an angle of 75° toward the right shoulder.

5.   FIG. 65.   The shorter of the two remaining flowers is placed in front toward the viewer. Its leaves should only partly cover the edge of the container. This is the most important flower for concealing the needle-point holder. It is also the focal point of the arrangement.

6.   PLATE 86.   To complete the arrangement, the remaining flower is placed slightly to the right and to the rear of the previous flower; it should incline toward the viewer. The needle-point holder should not be visible from any angle. Care should be taken to see that the leaves are in a somewhat horizontal position to their stems. They should not droop nor should they stand too vertical to their stems.

7.   FIG. 66.   A bird's-eye view of the positions of the three main branches.

FIG. 66

PLATE 86. BASIC LESSON 1

Fig. 67

Lesson 2. Moribana. Basic Slanting Style.

Material: *Japanese flowering quince.*

1. Fig. 67. As the container is long and narrow, the *shin* or primary stem is approximately the length plus the height of the container. The *soe* or secondary stem is three-quarters the length of the *shin*. The *hikae* or tertiary stem is three-quarters the length of the *soe*. The three short stems constitute *jûshi* or supporting flowers. Here, as they are to be placed at the base of the arrangement, they are all shorter than the *hikae*.

2. Fig. 68. The needle-point holder may be placed either to the left or the right of the container. The *shin* is placed at an angle of 45° toward the left shoulder.

3. Fig. 69. The *soe* is placed at an angle of 15° toward the left shoulder.

4. Fig. 70. The *hikae* is placed at an angle of 75° toward the right shoulder.

5. Plate 87. The arrangement is completed by placing the short stems at the base of the arrangement. The edge of the container should be covered a little, and the needle-point holder should not be visible.

6. Fig. 71. A bird's-eye view of the positions of the three main branches.

This form differs from the upright style of Lesson 1 in that the positions of the *shin* and *soe* have been reversed

Fig. 68

Fig. 69

PLATE 87. BASIC LESSON 2

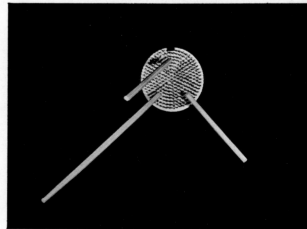

FIG. 70   FIG. 71

Basic Lessons   157

FIG. 72

PLATE 88.   BASIC LESSON 3

FIG. 73   FIG. 74.   FIG. 75

LESSON 3. MORIBANA. UPRIGHT STYLE, FIRST
           VARIATION.

Material: lilac and Solomon's seal.

1. FIG. 72. The long branch of lilac is the *shin,* its
length being approximately twice the length plus the
height of the container. The *soe* is three-quarters the
length of the *shin,* while the *hikae* is three-quarters the
length of the *soe.* The remaining four branches comprise the mass or fill-in branches *(jûshi);* all of these are
a little shorter than the *hikae.* As stated before, there is
no set rule for the length of these branches; however,
they should not exceed the length of the branch they
support.

2. FIG. 73. The *shin* is placed at an angle of 15° to
the right rear.

3. FIG. 74. The *soe* is placed at an angle of 45°
toward the left shoulder.

4. FIG. 75. The *hikae* is placed at an angle of 75°
toward the right shoulder. It will be noted that the
leaves on the lower right part of the stem have been
removed to avoid cluttering the edge of the container.

5. FIG. 76. One branch of lilac and one of Solomon's seal are placed at the base of the arrangement
and slightly cover the edge of the container.

6. PLATE 88. The arrangement is completed by
placing the remaining two branches of lilac and Solomon's seal to the rear of the arrangement in support of
the *shin.* Again, the needle-point holder should not be
visible. This form differs from the Basic Upright Style
in that the *shin* inclines at an angle of 15° to the right
rear instead of toward the left shoulder. A variation is
accomplished by reversing the *shin* and *soe,* thus creating a slanting style. The fill-in branches are changed
around at the discretion of the arranger to suit the
shin and *soe* branches.

7. FIG. 77. A bird's-eye view of the positions of the
three main branches.

FIG. 76

FIG. 77

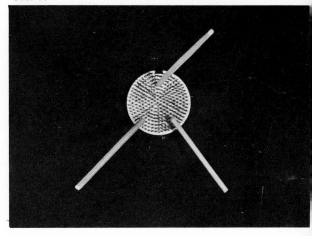

Fig. 78

Fig. 79

Fig. 80

LESSON 4. MORIBANA. UPRIGHT STYLE, SECOND
VARIATION.

Material: pussy willow and camellias.

1. FIG. 78. The length of the *shin* or primary branch
is approximately twice the width, plus the height, of the
container. The *soe* or secondary branch is three-quarters
the length of the *shin,* the *hikae* or tertiary branch three-
quarters the length of the *soe.* The camellias serve as
fill-in flowers at the base, and all are shorter than the
hikae. All of the three main branches are supported by
additional branches which are shorter than the branch
they support. There is no limit to the number of supporting branches one may use. This is usually decided
by the type of material.

2. FIG. 79. The *shin* is placed at an angle of 15°
toward the left shoulder and is supported by two
branches, one each to its front and rear. The needle-
point holder is placed to the left front of the container,
and as the container is made of glass the holder has
been covered with white paper. This makes it easier
for the holder to be concealed from view.

3. FIG. 80. The *soe* is placed at an angle of 75° toward the right shoulder and is supported by one
branch to its rear.

4. FIG. 81. The *hikae* is placed at an angle of 45°
toward the left shoulder and is supported by one
branch to its rear.

FIG. 81

FIG. 82

5. PLATE 89. The arrangement is completed by
placing the camellias at the base of the arrangement.
The needle-point holder should be completely hidden
from view. This form differs from the basic upright
style in that the positions of the *soe* and *hikae* are reversed. A variation can be made by reversing the positions of the *shin* and *hikae.* That is to say, the *shin* would
incline at an angle of 45° toward the left shoulder, the
hikae at an angle of 15° toward the left shoulder.

6. FIG. 82. A bird's-eye view of the positions of the
three main branches.

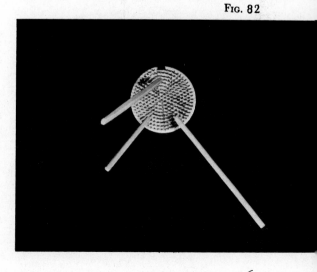

PLATE 89. BASIC LESSON 4

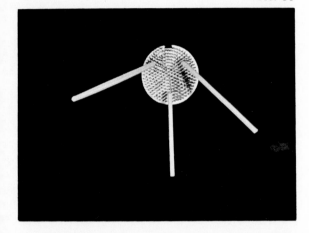

FIG. 83

FIG. 84

LESSON 5. MORIBANA. UPRIGHT STYLE, THIRD VARIATION.

Material: three roses.

1. FIG. 83. The length of the *shin* stem is the length plus the height of the container. The *soe* stem is three-quarters the length of the *shin;* the *hikae* stem, three-quarters the length of the *soe.* As the container is made of glass, the needle-point holder is wrapped in white tissue paper; this aids considerably in concealing the holder from view.

2. PLATE 90. The *shin* inclines at an angle of 15° toward the left shoulder, the *soe* at an angle of 45° toward the right shoulder, and the *hikae* at an angle of 75° directly toward the viewer. In this form of arrangement, the *hikae* is inserted in the holder first. A few leaves should cover the edge of the container and care should be exercised to eliminate unnecessary leaves. Too many leaves or leaves which are too large will spoil the arrangement.

3. FIG. 84. A bird's-eye view of the positions of the three main branches.

A slanting-style variation can be made by reversing the positions of the *shin* and *soe.* That is to say, the *shin* is placed at an angle of 45° to the right front, the *soe* at 15° to the left front, while the *hikae* remains unchanged.

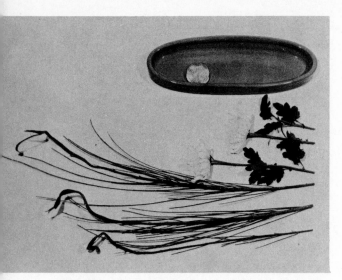

FIG. 85

FIG. 86 .

FIG. 87

LESSON 6. MORIBANA. UPRIGHT STYLE, FOURTH VARIATION.

Material: broom and chrysanthemums.

1. FIG. 85. This form of arrangement consists of only two of the usual three branches: a *shin* and a *hikae*. No *soe* is used. In this arrangement, two supporting branches have been used with the *shin*. As explained before, any of the main branches may have supporting branches but they should not be longer than the branch they support. One tall branch or leaf of any kind of material can be effectively used. The length of the *shin* is one and a half times the length, plus the height, of the container. The length of the chrysanthemum *hikae* remains in the same ratio as though a *soe* were used. The short chrysanthemum and leaves are to be placed at the base of the arrangement; hence they are shorter than the *hikae*.

2. FIG. 86. The *shin* is placed at an angle of 15° toward the left shoulder and is supported by the two shorter branches of broom. This branch may also be placed at an angle of 15° to the right rear.

3. PLATE 91. The arrangement is completed by placing the chrysanthemum *hikae* at an angle of 75° toward the right shoulder, and by placing the remaining flower at the base of the arrangement. The short stem of leaves is placed to the rear to give depth to the arrangement. The lip of the container is only lightly covered with leaves.

4. FIG. 87. A bird's-eye view of the positions of the two main branches.

A slanting-style variation may be made by inclining the *shin* at 45° toward the left shoulder, the *hikae* remains unchanged.

PLATE 91. *Basic Lessons* 6

Fig. 88

Fig. 89

Fig. 90

Lesson 7. Moribana. Upright Style, Fifth Variation.

Material: enkianthus and small chrysanthemums.

1. Fig. 88. This style of arrangement is done in two parts. The *shin* and the *soe* are placed in one holder, the *hikae* in another. The long *shin* is one and one-half times the length, plus the height, of the container. The *soe* is three-quarters the length of the *shin* and, because of the sparseness of its leaves, has a supporting branch. The four stems of small chrysanthemums comprise the *hikae,* the longest of which is three-quarters the length of the *soe.*

2. Fig. 89. The needle-point holder is placed to the left front of the container. The *shin* inclines at an angle of 15° toward the left shoulder.

3. Fig. 90. The *soe* is placed to the front of the *shin* and at an angle of 45° toward the left shoulder.

4. Plate 92. The arrangement is completed by placing the small chrysanthemum *hikae* branches at an angle of 75° toward the right shoulder in a needle-point holder placed to the right rear of the container. The position of the needle-point holders may be reversed by placing the *shin* and *soe* to the left rear and the *hikae* to the right front.

5. Fig. 91. A bird's-eye view of the positions of the main branches. The slanting-style variation is made by reversing the *shin* and *soe;* that is to say, the *shin* inclines at an angle of 45° toward the left shoulder, the *soe* at an angle of 15° toward the left shoulder. The *hikae* remains unchanged. For the slanting style, the *shin* and *soe* are placed to the left rear and the *hikae* to the right front.

A further variation may be made by using only short material in both needle-point holders.

Fig. 91

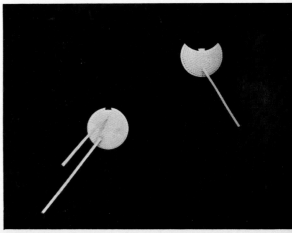

PLATE 92. BASIC LESSON 7

PLATE 93. BASIC LESSON 8

FIG. 92

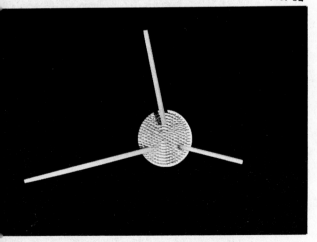

LESSON 8. MORIBANA. FLAT STYLE.

Material: gerberas and asparagus fern.

1. PLATE 93. This style of arrangement is viewable from all angles and is most suitable as a table arrangement. It has three styles: upright, slanting, and flat. The arrangement shown here is in the flat style, since the *shin* (primary branch), *soe* (secondary branch), and *hikae* (tertiary branch) all extend horizontally from the needle-point holder. In the upright and slanting styles, the same procedure is followed as outlined in previous lessons with the exception that the arrangement must be viewable from all four sides; for these two styles it is preferable to use a deeper container, such as a basket or bowl.

2. FIG. 92. A bird's-eye view of the positions of the three main branches.

Lesson 9. Floating Arrangement.

Material: gladiolus.

PLATE 94.   This form of arrangement is distinguished by its plant material floating in water and consequently by the absence of a needle-point holder. The material may be placed either in mass or may float freely, to one side or at the center of the container, as desired. Almost any kind of floral material, either leaves or flowers, can be used effectively in this manner. In this particular arrangement three gladiolus flowers have been grouped together and float behind two gladiolus leaves. A floating arrangement is known as an *uki-bana.*

Another style of arrangement included in this category, but not illustrated here, is the "spreading" arrangement *(shiki-bana),* in which flowers and leaves are arranged directly on a table without a container, needle-point holder, or water. This form is suitable as a table arrangement for a short period only.

PLATE 94.   BASIC LESSON 9

LESSON 10. MORIMONO.

Material: hydrangea, peaches, and apple.

Plate 95. A *morimono* is an arrangement of fruit, fruit and flowers, fruit and vegetables, vegetables, or vegetables and flowers. The arrangement shown here. has been made on the upturned lid of a basket. The arrangement may be made in or on almost any kind of container, be it bowl, basket, mat, straw, lid, or large natural leaf, such as banana or lotus leaf.

A *morimono* differs from a "spreading" arrangement, as described in the preceding lesson, in that its choice of materials is not restricted to flowers and that it is usually on a base of some sort.

PLATE 95. BASIC LESSON 10

FIG. 93

FIG. 94

Lesson 11. Moribana. Two-container Arrangement.

Material: leucothoe and gerberas.

This effective and versatile style is made by combining any two basic styles, in this instance the basic upright style (Lesson 1) and the slanting style (Lesson 5). Another striking arrangement is obtained by combining a hanging *nageire* style with a *moribana* style, that is, a tall vase with a hanging arrangement is placed to the rear of a low *moribana* arrangement. From this basic style many beautiful combinations can be developed.

1. Fig. 93. Two branches of leucothoe, three gerberas, and two gerbera leaves are used for the left container, while one branch of leucothoe, three gerberas, and one gerbera leaf are used for the right. The branch of leucothoe on the far left is the *shin* or primary branch; its length is governed by the placement of the two containers. The length of the *shin* in the arrangement on the right is the same as that of the *soe* (secondary branch) in the left-hand container.

2. Fig. 94. The *shin* for the right-hand container is placed at an angle of 45° toward the right shoulder.

3. Fig. 95. The *soe* is placed at an angle of 15° toward the left shoulder, and the branch of leucothoe forming the *hikae* is placed at an angle of 75° to the front. The length of the *soe* is three-quarters the length of the *shin,* that of the *hikae* three-quarters the length of the *soe.*

4. Fig. 96. The right-hand arrangement is completed by placing the remaining gerbera and gerbera leaf at its base. The *shin* of the left-hand arrangement is placed at an angle of 15° toward the left shoulder. Its length is approximately the distance between the outside edges of the two containers plus the height of one container.

FIG. 95

FIG. 96

Fig. 97

Fig. 98

5. Fig. 97. The *soe* of the left-hand arrangement is placed at an angle of 45° toward the left shoulder. As mentioned before, the length of this branch is the same as that of the *shin* in the right arrangement.

6. Fig. 98. The *hikae* or tertiary branch is placed at an angle of 75° toward the right shoulder.

7. Plate 96. The arrangement is completed by placing the remaining two gerberas and leaves at the base.

8. Fig. 99. A bird's-eye view of the positions of the three main branches in each needle-point holder.

Fig. 99

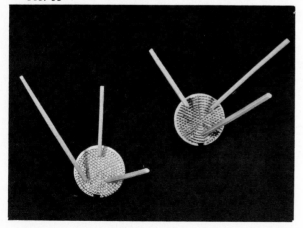

PLATE 96. BASIC LESSON 11

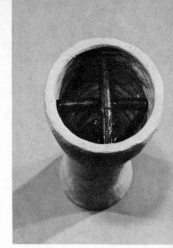

FIG. 100   FIG. 101

LESSON 12.   NAGEIRE.   BASIC UPRIGHT STYLE.

Material: three branches of Japanese plum and two gerberas.

Nageire, which is one of the oldest forms of Japanese flower arrangement, differs from *moribana* in two important aspects. First, a tall container is used instead of the low flat container used in *moribana;* secondly, no needle-point holder is used. In the old form of *nageire,* only two principal branches were used, and the mouth of the container was left free of any foliage for a height of several inches just as in the classical arrangements given earlier in this book. Modern *nageire,* however, follows the same basic principles of *moribana;* that is, three principal branches are used and foliage is used at the mouth or lip of the container.

1.   FIG. 100.   The length of the *shin* (primary branch) is approximately twice the height plus the width of the container. That of the *soe* (secondary branch) is three-quarters the length of the *shin.* That of the *hikae* (tertiary branch) is three-quarters the length of the *soe.*

The two gerberas used for fill-ins *(jûshi)* are shorter than the *hikae.*

2.   FIG. 101.   Two twigs are placed criss-cross in the mouth of the container, forming four quadrants. This enables the branches to stay in place without falling down into the container.

3.   FIG. 102.   The *shin* is placed at an angle of 15° toward the left shoulder. It is placed in the top right quadrant with the tip of the stem resting against the wall of the container.

4.   FIG. 103.   The *soe* is placed in the same quadrant as the *shin,* but at an angle of 45° toward the left shoulder.

5.   FIG. 104.   The *hikae* is also placed in the same quadrant as the *shin* and *soe,* but at an angle of 75° toward the right shoulder.

FIG. 102   FIG. 103

FIG. 104

6. PLATE 97. The arrangement is completed by placing the two gerberas at the base of the arrangement, one to the rear of the other to give depth. Foliage only partially covers the lip of the container.

A slanting-style *nageire* may be made by reversing the *shin* and *soe*. That is to say, the *shin* is placed at 45° toward the left shoulder, the *soe* at a 15° angle also toward the left shoulder.

FIG. 105

Material: rhòdodendron and chrysanthemums.

1. FIG. 105. The principal feature of this arrangement is that, in place of the criss-cross twigs used in the previous lesson, the *shin* is lengthened by splitting its end and inserting another split branch into it. The length of the *shin* with this extension is approximately twice the height plus the width of the container. As in all previous arrangements, the *soe* is three-quarters the length of the *shin,* and the *hikae* is three-quarters the length of the *soe*. The fill-in flowers are shorter than the *hikae.*

2. FIG. 106. The method of lengthening the *shin,* which is readily adaptable to the type of material and container used is clearly illustrated.

3. FIG. 107. The *shin* is inclined slightly toward the left shoulder.

4. FIG. 108. The *soe* stands out from, and hangs down the front of, the container.

5. FIG. 109. The *hikae* is placed to the rear of the *shin,* slightly inclined to the right shoulder.

6. FIG. 110. One fill-in chrysanthemum is placed below and slightly to the left of the *hikae.*

FIG. 106

FIG. 107

PLATE 98. BASIC LESSON 13

FIG. 108   FIG. 109   FIG. 110

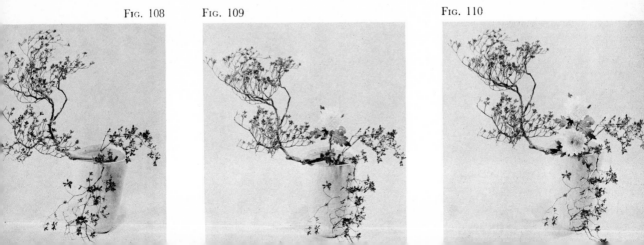

Fig. 111

LESSON 14. NAGEIRE. UPRIGHT STYLE.

*Material: Japanese pampas grass and
Chinese bellflower.*

As in the *moribana* described in Lesson 6, this form
of *nageire* employs only a *shin* and a *hikae*.

1. FIG. 111. The *shin* is placed 15° toward the left
front. The gourd-shaped basket is the same as is used
in the classical wall arrangement of Plate 29. Since the
bamboo water container is very narrow, the stick of
pampas grass rests near the mouth of the container.

2. PLATE 99. The arrangement is completed by
placing the Chinese bellflower at an angle of 45° toward the right shoulder; the end of its stem has been
bent slightly with the fingers to enable it to lean on the
lip of the container.

PLATE 99.   BASIC LESSO

LESSON 15. NAGEIRE. HANGING OR CASCADE STYLE.

*Material: dried gypsophila sprayed yellow
and red star lilies.*

PLATE 100.   This style of *nageire* features a hanging *shin* branch which falls below a horizontal line drawn through the mouth of the container. In this way it differs from the slanting style of *nageire,* in which the *shin* inclines at an angle of approximately 45° to the left shoulder. In the arrangement illustrated here, the container is tall (twenty-one inches) and the *shin* hangs nearly all the way down its side. Two long stems of lilies are arranged in support of the *shin,* and other lilies are massed at the base of the arrangement to give it vitality. As illustrated in Lesson 12, crossed twigs are placed near the mouth of the container to hold the material in place. If three distinct branches are used, the *shin* hangs down the side of the container, the *soe* is placed to the top left or right rear or front, and the *hikae* hangs down the front or slightly to the left or right of the front of the container.

This form is suitable for a tall container or for an arrangement which is to be placed above eye level.

PLATE 100.   BASIC LESSON 15

~ Appendix 1 ~

Preservation of Plants

THE CARE and preservation of cut flowers and foliage has always constituted an essential part of the study of Japanese floral art, for each flower, stem, and leaf stands silhouetted in the over-all design and therefore demands individual attention. Not only is it economical to have an arrangement last as long as possible, but in a country where exhibitions customarily last for from three to six days it is imperative that the arrangements retain their freshness throughout the entire period of the exhibition. From the early *rikka*-style arrangements in the 15th century to the present contemporary free forms numerous methods of treatment have evolved. To the Japanese these methods are known collectively as *mizu-age,* literally "water raising," an appropriate term, for most techniques are designed to stimulate the water-conductive cells of the plant after it has been cut.

Among the techniques most commonly used the following are worthy of special attention:

1. MIZU-GIRI (Fig. 112). This term means literally "water cutting" or, as practiced, the cutting of the stem while it is immersed in water. This is the most commonly used and the most effective of all the techniques. It seals the stem from absorbing air and is generally used for all plants irrespective of other methods which may be applied later. For some plants this method alone is considered adequate. Many plants require no treatment at all; in case of doubt, however, it is better to apply this method.

2. USE OF THE WATER PUMP (Fig. 113). In the case of such plants as the water lily and its leaves and the leaves of the lotus and yellow water lily, water or other recommended solution (see list at the end of this appendix) should be forced very slowly into the stem with a water pump until the flower or leaf is completely filled. To prevent the end of a stem from breaking, wrap a small piece of paper around it before inserting it into the nozzle of the pump.

3. INCREASING THE AREA OF ABSORPTION (Fig. 114). This is most effectively accomplished in one of three ways: (1) Cutting the stem on a slant. This is the general rule for cutting all plant material, as it not only increases the water-absorption area, but also facilitates insertion into needle-point holders. (2) Splitting the stem into four parts. This method is primarily used for woody material such as the plum or loquat. (3) Crushing the end of the stem. This

technique is applied to fibrous stems such as those of the chrysanthemum or hydrangea.

4. BURNING THE STEMS (Fig. 115). The stems of plants which exude a milky substance when cut, such as the poinsettia, should be held over an open flame which is as hot as possible in order that the period of burning may be kept to a minimum. The leaves and flowers should be protected by wrapping in damp paper or cloth. A similar effect may be obtained by immersing the stems in boiling water, but in some instances the burning method is more effective.

5. USE OF BOILING WATER. First immerse the stems in boiling water, whether fresh or salt, and then dip immediately into cold water.

6. USE OF CHEMICALS. Chemicals are used in varying degrees by the different schools. When using any chemical the general procedure is first to cut the stem while it is immersed in water, then to dry the stem, and finally to apply the chemical. The most commonly used chemicals are peppermint oil, tincture of capsicum, and alcohol. Hydrochloric acid is recommended for some plants, but care must be exercised in its use. It should not be used in metal containers or in places where house pets are apt to drink from the flower containers. The plant should be dipped in the acid for two or three seconds.

All plants should be in a healthy state before any of the foregoing treatments are applied. Most plants can be effectively revitalized by either (1) cutting the stems while immersed in water, sprinkling the leaves, and then standing them in fairly deep water, or (2) sprinkling the underside of the leaves with water and then wrapping them in damp newspaper. In either case, the plants should then be kept for several hours in a cool, dark place. This method is particularly effective for plants which have been transported for a long period of time.

Plants which are cut from the garden should be cut in the cool of the day, either early in the morning or in the evening, and then placed in water to a depth equal to at least one-third the length of the stems and left in a cool dark place until required. Sprinkle or spray the leaves with water. The technique of cutting the stems while immersed in water should be applied immediately after taking them from the garden and then repeated at the time of doing the arrangement. In Japanese flower arrangement, flowers are often arranged in very shallow water. If freshly cut flowers show signs of wilting after they have been arranged, they can be revived by recutting the stems while immersed in water and then leaving them overnight in water to a depth of at least one-third the length of the stems. As the leaves play an important part in the arrangements, care should be taken to ensure that the plants are not unnecessarily defoliated. However, when making the arrangement care should also be exercised to ensure that the immersed part of the stem is completely defoliated, otherwise the leaves will foul the water.

The following list shows which of the methods discussed above are used in

FIG, 112. Cutting a stem in water.

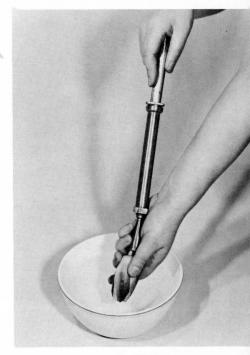

FIG. 113. Injecting liquid into a water lily by means of a pump.

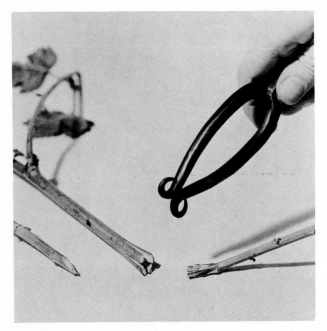

FIG. 114. From left to right: *1)* a stem cut on the slant, *2)* a stem split into four parts, and *3)* a stem crushed by hitting it with scissors.

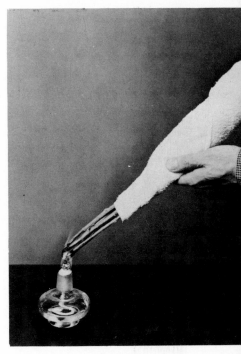

FIG. 115. Burning the stems. The flowers are protected by a damp cloth or paper.

varying degrees in Japan with specific flowers. Methods indicated after numbers in parentheses are alternatives; they are not listed in any order of preference, as practice alone will determine which of two or more methods is the most effective.

Acacia — Split the cut end into four parts and dip in peppermint oil for 2 or 3 seconds.

Aconite — Dip in peppermint oil for 4 or 5 seconds.

Agapanthus — Cut in water.

Akebia — Cut in water.

Amaranthus — Dip in a strong solution of boiling salted water containing 4 or 5 drops of peppermint oil for 4 or 5 seconds. Salted water without peppermint oil may also be used.

Amaryllis — Cut in water.

Anemone — Cut in water.

Anil — Dip in peppermint oil for 2 or 3 seconds.

Anthurium — No treatment needed.

Arum lily — Cut in water; inject water into the leaves by means of a pump.

Aspidistra — Cut in water.

Aster — Dip in peppermint oil, tincture of capsicum, or alcohol for a few seconds.

Azalea — Cut in water.

Balsam — (1) Split the cut end and dip in tincture of capsicum for a few seconds. (2) Dip in peppermint oil for a few seconds.

Bamboo — After bamboo has been cut it will not draw up water. To overcome this, drill or pierce a hole down through the center of the main branch to the bottom node, then fill with water. If this is not possible, pierce a small hole under each node and insert water into each section.

Banana plant — Dip in acetic acid for 5 or 6 seconds.

Begonia — Cut in water.

Bleeding heart — Split the cut end, then dip in tincture of capsicum for a few seconds.

Bougainvillea — Dip in peppermint oil for a few seconds.

Boxthorn — Dip in peppermint oil for 1 or 2 seconds.

Broom — No treatment needed.

Burnet — (1) Burn the cut end. (2) Dip in peppermint oil for 2 or 3 seconds.

Bush clover — (1) Rub salt into the cut end and then burn. (2) Dip in peppermint oil for 2 or 3 seconds.

Caladium — Rub salt into the cut end.

Calendula — Cut in water.

California poppy — Dip in peppermint oil or tincture of capsicum for 2 or 3 seconds.

Calla lily — Cut in water; inject water into the leaves by means of a pump.

Camellia — To prevent the flowers from falling, apply damp salt to the base of the stamens by means of a match or other such implement.

Canna — Dip in alcohol or peppermint oil for 2 or 3 seconds.

Carnation — Cut in water.

Caryopteris — Dip in peppermint oil for 2 or 3 seconds.

Castor-oil plant — Cut in water.

Cattail — No treatment needed.

Cattleya — Cut in water.

Celosia — Cut in water.

China aster — Split the cut end and dip in peppermint oil for 2 or 3 seconds.

Chinese agrimony — Dip in peppermint oil or tincture of capsicum for about 5 seconds.

Chinese bellflower — Crush the cut end for about $\frac{1}{2}$ inch and dip in vinegar or peppermint oil for 2 or 3 seconds.

Chinese lantern — Dip in tincture of capsicum for about 5 seconds.

Christmas rose — Cut in water.

Chrysanthemum — The methods for preserving the chrysanthemum are many and varied. The greatest problem is to preserve the leaves, which invariably wilt before the flowers. Accordingly, irrespective of which of the following methods is used, it is common practice to sprinkle the underside of the leaves with water. (1) Break the stem with the fingers and crush the broken end. (2) Split the cut end about $\frac{1}{2}$ inch and dip in peppermint oil for 1 or 2 seconds. (3) Burn the cut end. (4) Dip in hot water, alcohol, or tincture of capsicum for 4 or 5 seconds. (5) Crush the cut end about $\frac{1}{2}$ inch and rub salt or bicarbonate of soda into it. (6) Dip in boiling salted water for a few seconds.

Cineraria — (1) Crush the cut end and rub salt or bicarbonate of soda into it. (2) Dip in tincture of capsicum or peppermint oil for 2 or 3 seconds.

Clematis — Cut in water.

Clivia — Cut in water.

Columbine — Dip in alcohol or tincture of capsicum for 4 or 5 seconds.

Convolvulus — Dip in alcohol or tincture of capsicum for 3 or 4 seconds.

Cornflower — See page 244 on the use of hydrochloric acid.

Cosmos — (1) Rub salt into the cut end. (2) Dip in peppermint oil for a few seconds.

Cyclamen — Rub salt into the cut end.

Cymbidium — Cut in water.

Dahlia — (1) Dip in boiling water for a few seconds. (2) Crush the cut end slightly and dip in alcohol, peppermint oil, or tincture of capsicum for a few seconds.

Dendrobium — No treatment needed.

Deutzia — Dip in peppermint oil for 2 or 3 seconds.

Dogwood — See page 244 on the use of hydrochloric acid.

Easter lily — No treatment needed.

Elaeagnus — Burn the cut end, then dip in alcohol for 2 or 3 seconds.

Elder — See page 244 on the use of hydrochloric acid.

Enkianthus — Dip in tincture of capsicum for 5 or 6 seconds.

Erica — Cut in water.

Eupatorium — Dip in tincture of capsicum for 2 or 3 seconds.

Evening primrose — Rub salt into the cut end.

Flax—Dip in peppermint oil for 1 or 2 seconds.
Foxglove—Dip in peppermint oil for 1 or 2 seconds.
Freesia—Cut in water.
Fuchsia—See page 244 on the use of hydrochloric acid.

Gardenia—(1) Burn the cut end. (2) Dip in alcohol or peppermint oil for a few seconds.
Gentian—(1) Dip in alcohol or peppermint oil for a few seconds. (2) Crush the cut end and dip in boiling water for a few seconds.
Geranium—Dip in peppermint oil for 2 or 3 seconds.
Gerbera—Dip in hot water, alcohol, or peppermint oil for a few seconds.
Gladiolus—Cut in water.
Globe amaranth—Dip in hot water or peppermint oil for 1 or 2 seconds.
Gloxinia—Dip in peppermint oil for 5 or 6 seconds.
Golden bell—Cut in water.
Great reed—Dip in alcohol, then immerse in deep water.
Gypsophila—Cut in water.

Hawthorn—Burn the cut end.
Herbaceous peony—(1) Burn the cut end, then dip in alcohol for a few seconds. (2) Dip in acetic acid for 1 or 2 minutes.
Hibiscus—No treatment needed.
Hilenium—Cut in water.
Hollyhock—Dip in boiling salted water for a few seconds.
Honeysuckle—Dip in peppermint oil for 1 or 2 seconds.
Hosta—Dip in peppermint oil for a few seconds.
Hyacinth—Cut in water.
Hydrangea—(1) Crush the cut end, then dip in alcohol or acetic acid for a few seconds. (2) Dip in boiling water or boiling salted water for a few seconds. (3) See page 244 on the use of hydrochloric acid.

Inula—Dip in peppermint oil for 1 or 2 seconds.
Iris—Cut in water.

Japanese quince—Split the cut end into four parts and dip in peppermint oil for a few seconds.
Jasmine—Dip in peppermint oil for 2 or 3 seconds.
Job's tears—Dip in peppermint oil for 3 or 4 seconds.

Kale—No treatment needed.
Knotweed—Dip in alcohol for a few seconds.
Kudzu—Dip in peppermint oil for 4 or 5 seconds.

Lantana—Dip in tincture of capsicum for about 5 seconds.
Larkspur—Dip in tincture of capsicum for about 4 seconds.
Liatris—Cut in water.
Ligustrum—Dip in tincture of capsicum for about 4 seconds.
Lilac—Cut in water.
Linden—Burn the cut end and then dip in tincture of capsicum for a few seconds.
Loosestrife—Split the cut end, then dip in peppermint oil for 2 or 3 seconds.
Loquat—Split the stem into four parts for about ½ inch and dip in peppermint oil or tincture of capsicum for a few seconds.

Lotus—By means of a pump inject into the stem a solution of any one of the following: (1) Tincture of capsicum. (2) Cooled strong tea. (3) Tobacco stock (this can be made by placing cigarette tobacco in a thin cloth and squeezing it in water). (4) Ginger root (boil grated ginger root and allow it to cool). (5) Gypsum (make a thin solution in boiling water and inject quickly; as the solution cools the leaves appear taut). After this plant has been cut it is preferable to keep it immersed in the same water in which it has been growing.
Lupine—Dip in tincture of capsicum for about 5 seconds.
Lychnis—Split the cut end, then dip in tincture of capsicum for a few seconds.
Lythrum—See page 244 on the use of hydrochloric acid.

Magnolia—(1) Burn the cut end. (2) See page 244 on the use of hydrochloric acid.
Mallow—Dip in peppermint oil for a few seconds.
Maple—(1) Split the cut end into four parts, rub salt well into it, and burn. (2) Split the cut end into four parts and dip into vinegar, tincture of capsicum, or alcohol for 3 or 4 seconds. (3) To prevent the leaves from curling, spray them with glycerine or a thin solution of sugar and water. (4) See page 244 on the use of hydrochloric acid.
Marguerite—Dip in hot water or tincture of capsicum for 4 or 5 seconds.
Marigold—Cut in water.
Marvel of Peru—Dip in tincture of capsicum for about 5 seconds.
Mesembryanthemum—Dip in peppermint oil for 1 or 2 seconds.
Michaelmas daisy—Cut in water.
Montbretia—Dip in alcohol or tincture of capsicum for about 5 seconds.
Morning-glory—(1) Rub salt into the cut end. (2) Dip in alcohol or ginger root solution for a few seconds.
Myrica—cut in water.

Nandina—No treatment needed.
Narcissus—Dip in alcohol for about 5 seconds.
Nasturtium—Dip in tincture of capsicum for about 5 seconds.
New Zealand flax—No treatment needed.

Osmanthus—Burn the cut end.

Pampas grass—To make fluffy, hold in front of a warm stove or radiator. Otherwise no treatment needed.
Pansy—Cut in water.
Patrinia—Crush the cut end and dip in peppermint oil for a few seconds.
Periwinkle—Dip in peppermint oil or tincture of capsicum for 3 or 4 seconds.
Petunia—Dip in tincture of capsicum for about 5 seconds.
Phlox—(1) Cut in water. (2) See page 244 on the use of hydrochloric acid.
Pine—See page 244 on the use of hydrochloric acid.
Pink—Cut in water.
Pitcher plant—Cut in water.
Plum—(1) Split the cut end into four parts, rub salt into it, and then burn. (2) If it has green leaves, dip in peppermint oil for a few seconds.

Poinsettia — (1) Burn the cut end well. (2) Dip in hot water or tincture of capsicum for about 4 seconds.

Pomegranate — (1) Split the cut end into four parts and dip in peppermint oil for 2 or 3 seconds. (2) Split the cut end and rub salt into it, then burn.

Poppy — Dip in peppermint oil for about 4 seconds.

Primrose — Cut in water.

Pussy willow — No treatment needed.

Rape — Cut in water.

Red star lily — Cut in water.

Reed — See page 244 on the use of hydrochloric acid.

Rhodea Japonica — No treatment needed.

Rodgersia — Cut in water.

Rose — (1) Burn the cut end. (2) Crush the cut end and rub salt into it or dip in alcohol for a few seconds.

Rose of Sharon — (1) Burn the cut end. (2) Split the cut end into four parts and dip in vinegar or peppermint oil for 5 or 6 seconds.

Rue — See page 244 on the use of hydrochloric acid.

Salvia — Dip in peppermint oil or tincture of capsicum for a few seconds.

Scabiosa — Cut in water.

Snapdragon — Dip in peppermint oil for a few seconds.

Snow willow — Crush the cut end and dip in peppermint oil for a few seconds.

Solomon's seal — Split the cut end about 1/2 inch and then dip in peppermint oil for 1 or 2 seconds.

Sophora — Dip in peppermint oil for a few seconds.

Spider's wort — See page 244 on the use of hydrochloric acid.

Spiraea — Dip in peppermint oil for 3 or 4 seconds.

Stauntonia — Cut in water.

St. John's wort — Burn the cut end.

Stock — Crush the cut end.

Stokesia — No treatment needed.

Stonecrop — Cut in water.

Strelitzia — No treatment needed.

Styrax — See page 244 on the use of hydrochloric acid.

Sumac — Burn the cut end, then dip in tincture of capsicum for a few seconds.

Sunflower — Dip in vinegar for a few seconds.

Sweet daphne — Dip in tincture of capsicum for a few seconds.

Sweet pea — Cut in water.

Tamarisk — Dip in peppermint oil for a few seconds.

Thermopsis — Dip in peppermint oil for 1 or 2 seconds.

Trachelospermum — Dip in peppermint oil for a few seconds.

Tree peony — Burn well, then dip in alcohol for a few seconds.

Tuberose — Cut in water.

Tulip — (1) Dip in alcohol for three or four seconds. (2) Rub salt into the cut end. To prevent the flower from opening too quickly, pinch the stem at the base of the flower with the fingers.

Verbena — See page 244 on the use of hydrochloric acid.

Water lily — By means of a pump, inject water into the stems of the leaves and the flowers. A solution of three-fourths water and one-fourth alcohol injected into the flower will prevent it from closing.

Weeping willow — No treatment needed.

Wisteria — (1) Dip in alcohol or peppermint oil for 3 or 4 seconds. (2) Rub salt into the cut end and then burn.

Yarrow — Dip in peppermint oil for a few seconds.

Yellow water lily — By means of a pump inject a one-percent solution of tannic acid into the leaves and the flowers.

Zinnia — Dip in peppermint oil for a few seconds.

∾ Appendix 2 ∾

Nomenclature of Plants

FOLLOWING is a list of plants referred to in this volume and/or commonly used in Japanese flower arrangement. A full entry shows (1) common English name, (2) botanical name, and, if used in Japan, (3) common Japanese name. Japanese names and alternate English names are entered with cross references to their respective full entries. The abbreviation "com." means "commonly known as."

aburana; see rape

acacia—Acacia Baileyana F. Mueller—*ginyō-akashia* or *hana-āchichōku; see* artichoke

aconite—Aconitum chinense Sieb.—*tori-kabuto*

actinidia—Actinidia arguta Planch.—*sarunashi* (com. *kokuwa* or *akazuru*)

adenanthera (red sandalwood tree)—Adenanthera pavonina L.

Adonis—Adonis amurensis Regele et Radde—*fukuju-sō* or *gan-jitsu-sō*

afurika suiren; see water lily (1)

agabansasu; see agapanthus

agapanthus—Agapanthus umbellatus L'Her.—*agabansasu*

airisu; see iris (2) and (8)

ajisai; see hydrangea (1)

akabana hitsuji-gusa; see water lily (3)

akabana-kunshi-ran; see clivia

aka-jinjā; see red ginger

aka-matsu; see pine (1)

aka-no-mamma; see knotweed

akashia; see acacia

akazuru; see actinidia

akebi; see akebia

akebia—Akebia quinata Decne.—*akebi*

aki-zakura; see cosmos

alder—Alnus japonica Sieb. et Zucc.—*han-no-ki*

ama; see flax

amaranthus—Amaranthus tricolor L.—*ha-geitō*

amaririsu; see amaryllis

amaryllis—Hippeastrum hybridum Hort.—*amaririsu*

amerika-sennō; see lychnis (1)

amigasa-yuri; see fritillaria

andromeda; *see* pieris

anemone—Anemone japonica Sieb. et Zucc.—*shūmei-giku*

anil—Indigofera pseudo-tinctoria Matsum.—*koma-tsunagi*

ansuryūmu; see anthurium

anthurium—Anthurium Andreanum Lind.—*ansuryūmu*

anzu; see apricot

aoi; see hollyhock

aoki; see aucuba

ao-mamushi-gusa; see arisaema

apple—Malus pumila Mill. var. dulcissima Koidz.—*ringo*

apricot—Prunus Armeniaca L. var. Ansu Maxim.—*anzu*

aralia—Aralia cordata Thunb.—*udo*

araragi; see Japanese yew

araseitō; see stock

areca (betel-nut palm)—Areca Catechu L.—*binrōju*

arisaema—Arisaema serratum Schott—*ao-mamushi-gusa* or *ten-nan-shō*

artichoke—Cynara Scolymus L.—*chōsen-azami* (com. *āchichōku*)

arum lily; *see* calla lily

asagao; see morning glory

asagi-zuisen; see freesia

asebi; see pieris

ashi; see reed

asparagus—Asparagus cochinchinensis Merr.—*kusasugi-kazura* or *tenmondō*

asparagus fern—Asparagus plumosus Baker—*asuparagasu*

aspidistra—Aspidistra elatior Blume—*haran*

asplenium (spleenwort)—Asplenium antiquum Makino—*ōtani-watari* or *tani-watari*

aster—(1) Aster Savatieri Makino—*miyama-yomena* or *miyako-wasure.* (2) A. tataricus L.—*shion* or *asutā.* (3) A. trinervius Roxb.—*no-kongiku* or *kon-giku.* (4) A. novi-belgii L. (New York aster)—*yūzen-giku.*

astilbe (false goatsbeard)—Astilbe japonica Gray—*awamori-shōma* or *awamori-sō*

asuparagasu; see asparagus fern

asutā; see aster (2)

atsumori-sō; see lady's slipper

aucuba (variegated laurel)—Aucuba japonica Thunb.—*aoki*

Australian native rose—Boronia serrulata Sm.

awa; see millet

awamori-shōma; see astilbe

awamori-sō; see astilbe

ayame; see iris (5)

azalea—(1) Rhododendron obtusum Planch.—*yama-tsutsuji* (com. *tsutsuji*). (2) R. lateritium Planch.—*satsuki-tsutsuji* or *satsuki.*

azami; see thistle

azuma-giku; see erigeron

baika-utsugi; see philadelphus
baimo; see fritillaria
balsam — Impatiens Balsamina L.—hōsenka
bamboo—(1) Phyllostachys edulis A. et C. Riv.—mōsō-chiku (com. take). (2) P. reticulata C. Koch—ma-dake (com. take). (3) Sasa Veitchii Rehd.—yakiba-zasa or kuma-zasa (com. sasa or take).
banana plant — Musa Basjoo Sieb. et Zucc.—bashō
bara; see rose
barberry; see berberis
bashō; see banana plant
begonia; see begonia
begonia — Begonia Evansiana Andr.—shūkaidō (com. begonia)
begonia rex — Begonia Rex Putz.—taiyō-begonia
belamcanda—Belamcanda chinensis DC.—hiōgi or daruma-hiōgi
bellflower — Campanula punctata Lam.—hotaru-bukuro
beni-bana; see carthamus
beni-bana-sarubiya; see salvia
benkei-sō; see sedum (1)
berberis (barberry) — Berberis Sieboldi Miq.—hebi-noborazu or betel-nut palm; see areca ⌊tori-tomarazu
bijo-zakura; see verbena
binan-kazura; see kadsura
binrōju; see areca
bird of paradise; see strelitzia
biwa; see loquat
biyō-yanagi; see hypericum (1)
blackberry; see rubus
bleeding heart — Dicentra spectabilis DC.—keman-sō
bletilla — Bletilla striata Reichb. fil.—shiran
blueberry; see vaccinium
bodaiju; see linden
boke; see Japanese quince
boku; see driftwood
Boston ivy (Japanese ivy) — Parthenocissus tricuspidata Planch
botan; see tree peony ⌊—tsuta
box — Buxus microphylla Sieb. et Zucc. var. suffruticosa Makino
boxthorn — Lycium chinense Mill.—kuko ⌊—tsuge
broom — Cytisus scoparius Link.—enishida
bulrush; see scirpus
burnet; see sanguisorba
bush clover — Lespedeza bicolor Turcz.—yama-hagi (com. hagi)

caladium — Caladium bicolor Vent.—ha-nishiki (com. karajūmu)
calendula — Calendula officinalis L.—tō-kinsen
California poppy — Eschscholzia californica Cham.—hanabishi-sō
calla lily (arum lily) — Zantedeschia aethiopica Spreng.—oranda-kaiu (com. kaiu) ⌈sō
caltha — Caltha sibirica Makino var. decumbens Makino—enkō-camellia — (1) Camellia japonica L.—tsubaki. (2) C. reticulata Lindl.—tō-tsubaki. (3) C. Sasanqua Thunb.—sazanka.
campion; see lychnis
canna — Canna indica L.—dandoku (com. kanna)
capsicum — Capsicum annuum L.—tōgarashi ⌈nēshon)
carnation — Dianthus Caryophyllus L.—oranda-sekichiku (com. kā-carthamus (safflower) — Carthamus tinctorius L.—beni-bana
caryopteris — Caryopteris incana Miq.—dangiku or ran-giku
castor-oil plant — Ricinus communis L.—tōgoma
cattail (reed mace) — Typha latifolia L.—gama

cattleya — Cattleya labiata Lindl.—katorea
celastrus — Celastrus orbiculatus Thunb.—tsuru-umemodoki
celosia (cockscomb) — Celosia cristata L.—keitō
cercis — Cercis chinensis Bunge—hana-zuhō or suō
chidori-sō; see delphinium ⌈ezo-giku)
China aster — Callistephus chinensis Nees.—satsuma-kongiku (com.
China root — Smilax China L.—sarutori-ibara or san-kirai
Chinese bellflower — Platycodon grandiflorum A.DC.—kikyō
Chinese lantern—Physalis Alkekengi L.—hōzuki
chloranthus—Chloranthus glaber Makino—senryō
chōsen-azami; see artichoke
Christmas rose — Helleborus niger L.—kurisumasu-rōzu
chrysanthemum—Chrysanthemum morifolium Ramat. var. sinense Makino—kiku
chuberōzu; see tuberose
chūrippu; see tulip
cineraria — Senecio cruentus DC.—fūki-giku (com. shineraria)
citrus (mandarin orange)—Citrus deliciosa Tenore.—kishū-mikan
clematis — Clematis florida Thunb.—tessen ⌊(com. mikan)
clethra (white alder) — Clethra barbinervis Sieb. et Zucc.—ryōbu
clivia (Kafir lily) — Clivia miniata Regel.—akabana-kunshi-ran
club moss; see lycopodium ⌊(com. kunshi-ran)
cockscomb; see celosia
columbine—Aquilegia flabellata Sieb. et Zucc.—odamaki
commelina—Commelina communis L.—tsuyu-kusa
convolvulus — Calystegia japonicus Thunb.—hirugao
cornflower—Centaurea Cyanus L.—yaguruma-giku
cornus (dogwood) — (1) Cornus controversa Hemsl.—mizuki. (2) C. Kousa Buerg.—yama-bōshi. (3) C. officinalis Sieb. et Zucc.—san-shuyu. ⌈Blume—ha-shibami
corylus (filbert) — Corylus heterophylla Fisch. var. Thunbergii
cosmos — Cosmos bipinnatus Cav.—aki-zakura (com. kosumosu)
crab apple — Malus micromalus Makino—kaidō ⌈jikkō
crape myrtle — Lagerstroemia indical L.—saru-suberi or hyaku-cryptomeria (Japanese cedar)—Cryptomeria japonica D. Don—sugi ⌈kuramen)
cyclamen — Cyclamen persicum Miller—kagaribi-bana (com. shi-

daffodil — Narcissus Pseudo-Narcissus L.—rappa-zuisen
dahlia — Dahlia pinnata Cav.—tenjiku-botan (com. daria)
dai-ō-matsu; see pine (4)
dai-ō-shō; see pine (4)
danchiku; see great reed
dandoku; see canna
dangiku; see caryopteris
dango-giku; see helenium
daphne—Daphne odora Thunb.—jinchōge
daria; see dahlia
daruma-hiōgi; see belamcanda ⌈dori-sō
delphinium (larkspur) — Delphinium Ajacis L.—hien-sō or chi-dendorobyūmu; see dendrobium ⌈dendorobyūmu)
dendrobium—Dendrobium nobile Lindl.—kōki-sekkoku (com.
desmodium—Desmodium Oldhami Oliv.—fuji-kanzō or fuji-kusa
deutzia—Deutzia crenata Sieb. et Zucc.—utsugi or u-no-hana
distylium—Distylium racemosum Sieb. et Zucc.—isunoki (com.
dōdan-tsutsuji; see enkianthus ⌊yusu)
dogwood; see cornus
driftwood—boku

Easter lily; *see* lilium (4)

edgeworthia — Edgeworthia papyrifera Sieb. et Zucc.—*mitsumata*

ego-no-ki; see styrax ⌈*gumi*)

elaeagnus — Elaeagnus pungens Thunb.—*nawashiro-gumi* (com.

elder — Sambucus Sieboldiana Blume—*niwatoko*

enishida; see broom

enkianthus — Enkianthus perulatus C.K. Schn.—*dōdan-tsutsuji*

enkō-sō; see caltha

enokoro-gusa; see foxtail

erigeron (fleabane) — Erigeron dubius Makino—*azuma-giku*

euonymus (spindle tree) — (1) Euonymus Sieboldiana Blume—
mayumi. (2) E. japonica Thunb.—*masaki*.

eupatorium — Eupatorium japonicum Thunb.—*hiyodori-bana* or

evening primrose ; *see* oenothera ⌊*yama-ran*

everlasting daisy — Helichrysum bracteatum Willd.—*mugiwara-
ezo-giku; see* China aster ⌊*giku*

ezo-matsu; see spruce

false goatsbeard; *see* astilbe

false spiraea ; *see* sorbaria

fatsia (Japanese aralia) — Fatsia japonica Decne. et Planch.—

fig marigold; *see* mesembryanthemum ⌊*yatsude*

filbert; *see* corylus

flax (linseed-oil plant) — Linum usitatissimum L.—*ama*

fleabane; *see* erigeron

four-o'clock; *see* marvel-of-Peru

foxglove — Digitalis purpurea L.—*kitsune-no-tebukuro* (com. *jigi-
foxtail* — Setaria viridis Beauv.—*enokoro-gusa* ⌊*tarisu*)

fragrant olive; *see* osmanthus

freesia — Freesia refracta Klatt.—*asagi-zuisen* (com. *furijia*)

fritillaria (fritillary) — Fritillaria Thunbergii Miq.—*amigasa-yuri*
or *baimo*

fuchsia — Fuchsia speciosa Hort.—*hyōtan-sō* or *fukusha*

fuji; see wisteria

fuji-bakama; see thoroughwort

fuji-kanzō; see desmodium

fuji-kusa; see desmodium

fuji-zuru; see wisteria vine

fūki-giku; see cineraria

fukuju-sō; see Adonis

fukusha; see fuchsia

fuller's teasel — Dipsacus fullonum L.—*rashakaki-gusa* or *oni-nabe-
funikkusu; see* phoenix ⌊*na*

funkia; *see* hosta

furijia; see freesia

futoi; see scirpus (1)

fuyō; see hibiscus

gābera; see gerbera

gaku-ajisai; see hydrangea (2)

gama; see cattail

gama-zumi; see viburnum (1)

ganjitsu-sō; see Adonis

ganpi; see lychnis (2)

gansoku; see matteuccia ⌈—*kanoko-sō*

garden heliotrope — Valeriana officinalis L. var. latifolia Miq.

gardenia — Gardenia jasminoides Ellis—*kuchinashi*

gekkakō; see tuberose

gentian — Gentiana scabra Bunge var. Buergeri Maxim.—*rindō*

geranium — Pelargonium zonale Ait.—*mon-tenjiku-aoi* (com. *tenjiku-aoi* or *zeranyūmu*)

gerbera — Gerbera Jamesonii Hook.—*gābera*

gibōshi; see hosta

ginger lily — Hedychium coronarium Koenig.—*shukusha* (com.

gin-mokusei; see osmanthus (1) ⌊*jinjā*)

ginyō-akashia; see acacia

gladiolus — Gladiolus gandavensis Van Houtt.—*gurajiorasu*

gleditsia — Gleditschia japonica Miq.—*saikachi*

gleichenia — Gleichenia glauca Hook.—*urajiro* (com. *shida*) ⌈*sō*

globe amaranth — Gomphrena globosa L.—*sennichi-kō* or *sennichi-

gloxinia — Sinningia speciosa Benth. et Hook. Fil.—*ōihagiri-sō*

gokuraku-chō; see strelitzia ⌊(com. *gurokishinia*)

golden bell — Forsythia suspensa Vahl—*rengyō*

golden-rayed lily; *see* lilum (1)

gourd — Lagenaria leucantha Rusby var. Gourda Makino—
goyō-matsu; see pine (2) ⌊*hyōtan*

great reed — Arundo Donax L. var. benghalensis Makino—*yoshi-
gumi; see* elaeagnus ⌊*take* (com. *danchiku*)

gurajiorasu; see gladiolus

gurokishinia; see gloxinia

gyoryū; see tamarisk ⌈*kasumi-sō; when dried, sutāchisu*)

gypsophila — Gypsophila paniculata L.—*kogome-nadeshiko* (com.

ha-botan; see kale

ha-geitō; see amaranthus

hagi; see bush clover

hagoromo-sō; see yarrow

hana-akashia; see acacia

hanabishi-sō; see California poppy

hana-shōbu; see iris (1)

hanatade; see knotweed

hana-zuhō; see cercis

ha-nishiki; see caladium

hankai-sō; see ligularia (2)

han-no-ki; see alder

haran; see aspidistra

hardy orange — Poncirus trifoliata Rafin.—*karatachi*

ha-shibami; see corylus

hasu; see lotus

hawthorn — Crataegus cuneata Sieb. et Zucc.—*sanzashi*

haze-no-ki; see sumac (2)

heavenly bamboo; *see* nandina

hebi-noborazu; see berberis

helenium — Helenium autumnale L.—*dango-giku* (com. *herenyūmu*)

helianthus (sunflower)—(1) H. annuus L. (common sunflower)
—*himawari*. (2) H. debilis Nutt.—*hime-himawari*.

henrūda; see rue

herbaceous peony — Paeonia albiflora Pall.—*shakuyaku*

herb of grace; *see* rue

herenyūmu; see helenium

hibiscus — Hibiscus mutabilis L.—*fuyō*

hien-sō; see delphinium

higan-bana; see lycoris

hiiragi; see osmanthus (2)

hiiragi-nanten; see mahonia

himawari; see helianthus (1)

hime-himawari; see helianthus (2)
hime-hiōgi-zuisen; see montbretia
hime-kobushi; see magnolia (6)
hime-komatsu; see pine (2)
hime-yuri; see lilium (2)
hina-geshi; see poppy (1)
hinoki; see Japanese cypress
hiōgi; see belamcanda
hirugao; see convolvulus
hitsuji-gusa; see water lily (4)
hiyashinsu; see hyacinth
hiyodori-bana; see eupatorium
hōki; see summer cypress
hōki-gi; see summer cypress
hokuro; see Japanese ground orchid
holcus—Holcus Sorghum L. var. japonicus Makino—*morokoshi*
holly; *see* ilex
hollyhock—Althaea rosea Cav.—*tachi-aoi* (com. *aoi*)
honeysuckle; *see* lonicera
hō-no-ki; see magnolia (5)
horsetail—Equisetum hiemale L. var. japonicum Milde.—*tokusa*
hōsenka; see balsam
hōso; see oak (3)   ⌈romena F. Maekawa—*gibōshi*
hosta (plantain lily, funkia)—Hosta undulata Bailey var. er-
hotaru-bukuro; see bellflower
hototogisu; see Japanese toad lily
hozaki-nanakamado; see sorbaria
hōzuki; see Chinese lantern
hyacinth—Hyacinthus orientalis L.—*hiyashinsu*
hyakujikkō; see crape myrtle
hyakunichi-sō; see zinnia
hyōtan; see gourd
hyōtan-sō; see fuchsia
hydrangea—(1) Hydrangea macrophylla Seringe var. Otaksa
    Makino—*ajisai.* (2) H. macrophylla Seringe—*gaku-ajisai.*
hypericum (St. John's wort)—(1) Hypericum chinense L.—
    biyō-yanagi. (2) H. patulum Thunb.—*kinshibai*

ibota-no-ki; see ligustrum
ibuki; see juniper
ichihatsu; see iris (7)
ichii; see Japanese yew
ilex (holly)—(1) Ilex integra Thunb.—*mochi-no-ki.* (2) I. serrata
inu-gansoku; see matteuccia   ⌊Thunb.—*umemodoki*
inula—Inula japonica Thunb.—*oguruma*
iris—(1) Iris ensata Thunb.—*hana-shōbu.* (2) I. holandica Hort.
    (Dutch iris)—*oranda-ayame* (com. *airisu*). (3) I. japonica Thunb.
    —*shaga.* (4) I. laevigata Fisch. (Japanese iris)—*kakitsubata.* (5)
    I. nertschinskia Lodd.—*ayame.* (6) I. Pseudacorus L. (yellow iris)
    —*ki-shōbu.* (7) I. tectorum Maxim.—*ichihatsu.* (8) I. Xiphium
    L. (Spanish iris)—*supein-ayame* (com. *airisu*).
isunoki; see distylium
iwa-nanten; see leucothoe

jakō-renri-sō; see sweet pea
Japan globeflower; *see* kerria   ⌈*rōbai*
Japanese allspice—Chimonanthus praecox Rehd. et Wilson—
Japanese aralia; *see* fatsia

Japanese cherry—Prunus serrulata Lindl.—*sakura*
Japanese chestnut—Castanea crenata Sieb. et Zucc.—*kuri*
Japanese cypress—Chamaecyparis obtusa Sieb. et Zucc.—*hinoki*
Japanese ground orchid—Cymbidium virescens Lindl.—*hokuro*
Japanese holly; *see* osmanthus (2)   ⌊or *shunran*
Japanese ivy; *see* Boston ivy   ⌈or *obana*
Japanese pampas—Miscanthus sinensis Anderss.—*kaya, susuki,*
Japanese plum—Prunus salicina Lindl.—*sumomo*
Japanese quince—Chaenomeles lagenaria Koidz.—*boke*
Japanese snowball; *see* viburnum (2)
Japanese storax; *see* styrax
Japanese toad lily—Tricyrtis hirta Hook.—*hototogisu*
Japanese Turk's-cap lily; *see* lilium (3)   ⌈*mansaku*
Japanese witch-hazel—Hamamelis japonica Sieb. et Zucc.—
Japanese yew—Taxus cuspidata Sieb. et Zucc.—*ichii* or *araragi*
jasmine—Jasminum grandiflorum L.—*sokei*
Jerusalem artichoke—Helianthus tuberosus L.—*kiku-imo*
Jew's mallow; *see* kerria
jigitarisu; see foxglove
jinchōge; see daphne
jinjā; see ginger lily
Job's tears—Coix Lachryma-Jobi L.—*juzu-dama*
juniper—Juniperus chinensis L.—*ibuki*
juzu-dama; see Job's tears

kadsura—Kadsura japonica Dunal.—*sane-kazura* or *binan-kazura*
kaede; see maple
kafir lily; *see* clivia
kagaribi-bana; see cyclamen
kaidō; see crab apple
kaiu; see calla lily
kaki; see persimmon
kakitsubata; see iris (4) ·
kale—Brassica oleracea L. var. capitata L.—*tamana* (com. *ha-*
kānēshon; see carnation   ⌊*botan*)
kangarei; see scirpus (3)
kanna; see canna
kanoko-sō; see garden heliotrope
kanzō; see yellow day lily
karaito-sō; see sanguisorba (1)
karajūmu; see caladium
karatachi; see hardy orange
kashiwa; see oak (2)
kasumi-sō; see gypsophila
katorea; see cattleya
kawa-yanagi; see pussy willow
kawara-nadeshiko; see pink.
kaya; see Japanese pampas
keitō; see celosia
keman-sō; see bleeding heart
kerria (Jew's mallow, Japan globeflower)—Kerria japonica DC.
keshi; see poppy (2)   ⌊—*yamabuki*
kibana-no-ha-uchiwa-mame; see lupine
ki-ichigo; see rubus
kiku; see chrysanthemum
kiku-imo; see Jerusalem artichoke
kikyō; see Chinese bellflower
kingyo-sō; see snapdragon

kinshibai; see hypericum (2)
kiri; see paulownia
kirin-giku; see liatris
kirin-sō; see sedum (2)
ki-shōbu; see iris (6)
kishū-mikan; see citrus
kitsune-no-tebukuro; see foxglove
knotgrass; *see* knotweed
knotweed (knotgrass) — Polygonum Blumei Meisn. — *hanatade,*
kobushi; see magnolia (4) ⌊*aka-no-mamma,* or *tade*
kodemari; see spiraea (2)
kogome-nadeshiko; see gypsophila
kōhone; see yellow water lily
kōki-sekkoku; see dendrobium
kokuwa; see actinidia
koma-tsunagi; see anil
kon-giku; see aster (3)
kosumosu; see cosmos
kōya-maki; see umbrella pine
kuchinashi; see gardenia
kudzu vine — Pueraria hirsuta Matsum.—*kuzu*
kuko; see boxthorn
kuma-zasa; see bamboo (3)
kunshi-ran; see clivia
kunugi; see oak (1)
kurara; see sophora
kuri; see Japanese chestnut
kurisumasu-rōzu; see Christmas rose
kuro-matsu; see pine (3)
kusa-kyōchikutō; see phlox
kusare-tama; see lysimachia (2)
kusasugi-kazura; see asparagus
kuzu; see kudzu
kyōchikutō; see oleander

lady's slipper — Cypripedium Thunbergii Blume—*atsumori-sō*
lantana — Lantana Camara L.—*rantana*
larkspur; *see* delphinium
leucothoe ☙—Leucothoe Keiskei Miq.—*iwa-nanten*
liatris — Liatris spicata Willd.—*kirin-giku* (com. *riatorisu*)
ligularia — (1) Ligularia tussilaginea Makino—*tsuwa-buki.* (2) L.
japonica Less.—*hankai-sō* ⌈Blume—*ibota-no-ki*
ligustrum (privet) — Ligustrum Ibota Sieb. var. angustifolium
lilac — Syringa vulgaris L.—*rairakku* or *rira*
lilium—(1) L. auratum Lindl. (golden-rayed lily)—*yoshino-yuri*
or *yama-yuri.* (2) L. concolor Salisb. var. Buschianum Baker
(red star lily)—*hime-yuri.* (3) L. Hansonii Leicht. (Japanese
Turk's-cap lily)—*takeshima-yuri.* (4) L. longiflorum Thunb.
(Easter lily)—*teppō-yuri.* ⌈*suzuran*
lily of the valley — Convallaria majalis L. var. Keiskei Makino—
linden — Tilia Miqueliana Maxim.—*bodaiju*
linseed-oil plant; *see* flax
lobelia — Lobelia sessilifolia Lamb.—*sawagikyō*
lonicera (honeysuckle) — (1) Lonicera japonica Thunb.—*suikazura* or *nindō.* (2) L. sempervirens L.—*tsukinuki-nindō*
loosestrife; *see* lysimachia
loquat — Eriobotrya japonica Lindl.—*biwa*
lotus — Nelumbo nucifera Gaertn.—*hasu*

lupine — Lupinus luteus L.—*kibana-no-ha-uchiwa-mame* (com. *rupinasu*)
lychnis (campion) — (1) Lychnis chalcedonica L.—*amerika-sennō.*
(2) L. coronata Thunb.—*ganpi.* (3) L. Senno Sieb. et Zucc.—
sennō ⌈*sugi*
lycopodium (club moss) — Lycopodium obscurum L.—*mannen-
lycoris* — Lycoris radiata Herb—*higan-bana* or *manju-shage*
lysimachia (loosestrife) — (1) Lysimachia clethroides Duby.—
oka-tora-no-o or *tora-no-o.* (2) L. vulgaris L. var. davurica R.
Knuth—*kusare-tama*
lythrum — Lythrum anceps Makino—*miso-hagi*

ma-dake; see bamboo (2)
māgaretto; see marguerite
magnolia — (1) Magnolia liliflora Desrouss—*mokuren.* (2) M.
parviflora Sieb. et Zucc.—*ōyama-renge* or *miyama-renge.* (3) M.
grandiflora L.—*taisan-boku.* (4) M. Kobus DC.—*kobushi.* (5)
M. obovata Thunb.—*hō-no-ki.* (6) M. stellata Maxim.—*shide-
kobushi* or *hime-kobushi*
mahonia — Mahonia japonica DC.—*hiiragi-nanten*
mallow — Malva sylvestris L. var. mauritiana Mill.—*zeni-aoi*
mandarin orange; *see* citrus
manju-shage; see lycoris
mannen-sugi; see lycopodium
mansaku; see Japanese witch-hazel
maple (Japanese maple) — Acer palmatum Thunb.—*takao-momiji*
(com. *momiji* or *kaede*) ⌈(com. *māgaretto*)
marguerite — Chrysanthemum frutescens L.—*moku-shungiku*
marvel-of-Peru (four-o'clock) — Mirabilis Jalapa L.—*oshiroi-bana*
masaki; see euonymus (2)
matsu; see pine
matsuba-giku; see mesembryanthemum
matsu-kasa-susuki; see scirpus (2)
matsumushi-sō; see scabiosa
matteuccia (ostrich fern) — Matteuccia orientalis Trev.—*inu-gan-
mayumi; see* euonymus (1) ⌊*soku* (com. *gansoku*)
me-matsu; see pine (1)
mesembryanthemum (fig marigold) — Mesembryanthemum
mikan; see citrus ⌊spectabile Haw.—*matsuba-giku*
millet — Setaria italica Beauv.—*awa*
miso-hagi; see lythrum
mitsumata; see edgeworthia
miyako-wasure; see aster (1)
miyama-naruko-yuri; see Solomon's seal
miyama-renge; see magnolia (2)
miyama-yomena; see aster (1)
mizu-aoi; see monochoria
mizuki; see cornus (1)
mochi-no-ki; see ilex (1)
mock orange; *see* philadelphus
mokuren; see magnolia (1)
mokusei; see osmanthus (1)
moku-shungiku; see marguerite
momiji; see maple
momiji-ichigo; see rubus
momo; see peach
monochoria — Monochoria Korsakowii Reg. et Maack.—*mizu-aoi*
monstera — Monstera deliciosa Liebm.—*monsutera*

monsutera; see monstera

montbretia — Tritonia crocosmaeflora Lemoine. —*hime-hiōgi-zuisen* (com. *montoburechia*)

mon-tenjiku-aoi; see geranium

montoburechia; see montbretia

morning-glory — Ipomoea hederacea Jacq. —*asagao*

morokoshi; see holcus

mōsō-chiku; see bamboo (1)

mube; see stauntonia

mugiwara-giku; see everlasting daisy

mukuge; see rose of Sharon

murasaki-omoto; see rhoeo

murasaki-tsuyukusa; see spiderwort

myrica — Myrica rubra Sieb. et Zucc. —*yama-momo*

nadeshiko; see pink

nanakamado; see sorbus

nandina (heavenly bamboo) — Nandina domestica Thunb.—

nanten; see nandina   ⌊*nanten*

nara; see oak (3)

narcissus — Narcissus Tazetta L. var. chinensis Roem. —*suisen*

nasturtium — Tropaeolum majus L. —*nōzenharen* (com. *nasutā-*

nasutāchūmu; see nasturtium   ⌊*chūmu*)

natane; see rape

natanena; see rape

natsu-haze; see vaccinium

nawashiro-gumi; see elaeagnus

neko-yanagi; see pussy willow

New York aster; *see* aster (4)

New Zealand flax — Phormium tenax Forst. —*nyūsai-ran*

nindō; see lonicera (1)

niwatoko; see elder

noda-fuji; see wisteria

no-kanzō; see yellow day lily

nokogiri-sō; see yarrow

no-kongiku; see aster (3)

nōzenharen; see nasturtium

.nurude; see sumac (1)

nyūsai-ran; see New Zealand flax

oak — (1) Quercus acutissima Carruth.—*kunugi*. (2) Q. dentata Thunb.—*kashiwa*. (3) Q. serrata Thunb.—*hōso* or *nara*.

obana; see Japanese pampas

odamaki; see columbine

ōdemari; see viburnum (2)

oenothera (evening primrose) — Oenothera tetraptera Cav.—

oguruma; see inula   ⌊*tsukimi-sō*

ōihagiri-sō; see gloxinia

oka-tora-no-o; see lysimachia (1)

oleander — Nerium indicum Mill. —*kyōchikutō*

o-matsu; see pine (3)

ominaeshi; see patrinia

omoto; see rhodea

oni-nabena; see fuller's teasel

oranda-ayame; see iris (2)

oranda-kaiu; see calla lily

oranda-sekichiku; see carnation

oshiroi-bana; see marvel-of-Peru

osmanthus (fragrant olive) — (1) O. fragrans Lour.—*mokusei* or *gin-mokusei*. (2) O. ilicifolius Mouillef (Japanese holly) —*hiiragi*.

ostrich fern; *see* matteuccia

ōtani-watari; see asplenium

otoko suiren; see water lily (2)

ōyama-renge; see magnolia (2)

palm — Trachycarpus excelsa Wendl. —*shuro*

pampas grass — Cortaderia argentea Stapf—*pampasu*

pampasu; see pampas grass

panji; see pansy

pansy — Viola tricolor L. —*sanshiki-sumire* (com. *panji*)

patrinia — Patrinia scabiosaefolia Link. —*ominaeshi*

paulownia — Paulownia tomentosa Steud. —*kiri*

peach — Prunus Persica Batsch. —*momo*

periwinkle — Vinca major L. —*tsuru-nichinichi-sō*

persimmon — Diospyros Kaki L. fil. —*kaki*

petunia — Petunia violacea Lindl. —*tsukubane-asagao*

philadelphus (mock orange)—Philadelphus satsumanus Sieb.—

phlox — Phlox paniculata L. —*kusa-kyōchikutō*   ⌊*baika-utsugi*

phoenix — Phoenix Roebelenii O'Brien—*shinōyashi* (com. *funik-*

pieris (andromeda) — Pieris japonica D. Don—*asebi*   ⌊*kusu*)

pine—(1) Pinus densiflora Sieb. et Zucc. (Japanese red pine)—*aka-matsu* or *me-matsu* (com. *matsu*). (2) P. pentaphylla Mayr. (five-needle pine)—*goyō-matsu* or *hime-komatsu* (com. *matsu*). (3) P. Thunbergii Parl. (Japanese black pine)—*kuro-matsu* or *o-matsu* (com. *matsu*). (4) P. australis Michx. (long-leaf pine)—*dai-ō-matsu* or *dai-ō-shō* (com. *matsu*).

pink — Dianthus superbus L. —*nadeshiko* or *kawara-nadeshiko*

pitcher plant — Nepenthes Rafflesiana Jack—*utsubo-kazura*

plane-tree; *see* platanus

plantain lily; *see* hosta   ⌈(com. *puratanasu*)

platanus (plane-tree) — Platanus orientalis L. —*suzukake-no-ki*

plum (botanically defined as Japanese flowering apricot) — Prunus Mume Sieb. et Zucc. —*ume*

plume poppy — Macleya cordata R. Br—*takeni-gusa*

podocarpus — Podocarpus chinensis Wall. —*rakan-maki*

poinsechia; see poinsettia

poinsettia — Poinsettia pulcherrima Graham—*shōjōboku* or *poin-*

pomegranate — Punica Granatum L. —*zakuro*   ⌊*sechia*

poppy—(1) Papaver Rhoeas L. —*hina-geshi*. (2) P. somniferum

primrose — Primula Sieboldi Morren—*sakura-sō*   ⌊L.—*keshi*.

privet; *see* ligustrum

puratanasu; see platanus   ⌈*yanagi*)

pussy willow — Salix gracilistyla Miq. —*kawa-yanagi* (com. *neko-*

rairakku; see lilac

rakan-maki; see podocarpus

ran-giku; see caryopteris

rantana; see lantana

rape — Brassica campestris L. subsp. Napus Hook. fil. et Anders. var. nippo-oleifera Makino—*aburana*, *natanena*, or *natane*

rappa-zuisen; see daffodil

rashakaki-gusa; see fuller's teasel

red ginger — Alpinia purpurata K. —*aka-jinjā*

red sandalwood tree; *see* adenanthera

red star lily; *see* lilium (2)

reed — Phragmites communis Trin. —*ashi* or *yoshi*

reed mace; *see* cattail
reng yō; see golden bell
rhodea —Rhodea japonica Roth—*omoto*
rhododendron—(1) R. Metternichii Sieb. et Zucc.—*shakunage.*
    (2) R. serpyllifolium Miq.—*unzen-tsutsuji.*
rhoeo—Rhoeo discolor Hance—*murasaki-omoto*
riatorisu; see liatris
rindō; see gentian
ringo; see apple
rira; see lilac
rōbai; see Japanese allspice
Rodger's bronze leaf; *see* rodgersia
rodgersia (Rodger's bronze leaf)—Rodgersia podophylla A.
    Gray—*yaguruma-sō*   ┌—com. *bara*
rose—Rosa Hybrid Tea (peace, golden rapture, happiness, etc.)
rose of Sharon—Hibiscus syriacus L.—*mukuge*   ┌*momiji-ichigo*
rubus (blackberry)—Rubus palmatus Thunb.—*ki-ichigo* or
rue (herb of grace)—Ruta graveolens L.—*henrūda*
rupinasu; see lupine
ruri-giku; see stokesia
ryōbu; see clethra

safflower; *see* carthamus
sago palm—Cycas revoluta Thunb.—*sotetsu*
saikachi; see gleditsia
sakura; see Japanese cherry
sakura-sō; see primrose
salvia—Salvia coccinea L.—*beni-bana-sarubiya* or *sarubiya*
sane-kazura; see kadsura
sanguisorba (burnet)—(1) Sanguisorba hakusanensis Makino
    —*karaito-sō.* (2) S. officinalis L.—*waremokō*
san-kirai; see China root
sanshiki-sumire; see pansy
san-shuyu; see cornus (3)
sanzashi; see hawthorn
sarubiya; see salvia
sarunashi; see actinidia
saru-suberi; see crape myrtle
sarutori-ibara; see China root
sasa; see bamboo (3)
satsuki; see azalea (2)
satsuki-tsutsuji; see azalea (2)
satsuma-kongiku; see China aster
sawagikyō; see lobelia
sazanka; see camellia (3)
scabiosa—Scabiosa japonica Miq.—*matsumushi-sō*
scirpus (bulrush)—(1) Scirpus lacustris L. var Tabernaemontani
    Trautv.—*futoi.* (2) S. Mitsukurianus Makino—*matsu-kasa-
    susuki.* (3) S. mucronatus L.—*kangarei.*
sedum (stonecrop)—(1) S. alboroseum Baker—*benkei-sō.* (2) S.
sendai-hagi; see thermopsis   └kamtschaticum Fisch.—*kirin-sō.*
sennichi-kō; see globe amaranth
sennichi-sō; see globe amaranth
sennō; see lychnis (3)
senryō; see chloranthus
shaga; see iris (3)
shakunage; see rhododendron (1)
shakuyaku; see herbaceous peony

shida; see gleichenia
shidare-yanagi; see weeping willow
shide-kobushi; see magnolia (6)
shikuramen; see cyclamen
shimo-tsuke; see spiraea (1)
shineraria; see cineraria
shinōyashi; see phoenix
shion; see aster (2)
shira-kaba; see white birch
shiran; see bletilla
shōjōboku; see poinsettia
shūkaidō; see begonia
shukusha; see ginger lily
shūmei-giku; see anemone
shunran; see Japanese ground orchid
shuro; see palm
snapdragon—Antirrhinum majus L.—*kingyo-sō*
snow willow; *see* spiraea (3)
sokei; see jasmine   ┌*naruko-yuri*
Solomon's seal—Polygonatum lasianthum Maxim.—*miyama-*
sophora—Sophora angustifolia Sieb. et Zucc.—*kurara*
sorbaria (false spiraea)—Sorbaria sorbifolia A. Br. var. stellipila
    Maxim.—*hozaki-nanakamado*
sorbus—Sorbus commixta Hedlund.—*nanakamado*
sotetsu; see sago palm
spiderwort—Tradescantia reflexa Rafin.—*murasaki-tsuyukusa*
spindle tree; *see* euonymus
spiraea—(1) Spiraea japonica L. fil.—*shimo-tsuke.* (2) S. can-
    toniensis Lour.—*kodemari.* (3) S. Thunbergii Sieb. (snow wil-
spleenwort; *see* asplenium   └low)—*yuki-yanagi.*
spruce—Picea jezoensis Carr.—*tōhi* (com. *ezo-matsu*)
stauntonia—Stauntonia hexaphylla Decne.—*mube*
St. John's wort; *see* hypericum
stock—Matthiola incana R. Br.—*araseitō* or *sutokku*
stokesia—Stokesia laevis Hill—*ruri-giku* (com. *sutokeshia*)
stonecrop; *see* sedum   ┌*raku-chō* or *sutorechiya*
strelitzia (bird of paradise)—Strelitzia Reginaea Banks.—*goku-*
styrax (Japanese storax)—Styrax japonica Sieb. et Zucc.—*ego-*
sugi; see cryptomeria   └*no-ki*
suikazura; see lonicera (1)
suiren; see water lily
suisen; see narcissus
suitopii; see sweet pea
sumac—(1) Rhus javanica L.—*nurude.* (2) R. trichocarpa Miq.—
sumire; see violet   └*haze-no-ki.*
summer cypress—Kochia scoparia Schrad.—*hōki-gi* (com. *hōki*)
sumomo; see Japanese plum
sunflower; *see* helianthus
suō; see cercis
supein-ayame; see iris (8)
susuki; see Japanese pampas
sutāchisu; see gypsophila
sutokeshia; see stokesia
sutokku; see stock
sutorechiya; see strelitzia
suzukake-no-ki; see platanus
suzuran; see lily of the valley
sweet pea—Lathyrus odoratus L.—*jakō-renri-sō* (com. *suitopii*)

tachi-aoi; see hollyhock
tade; see knotweed
taisan-boku; see magnolia (3)
taiyō-begonia; see begonia rex
takao-momiji; see maple
take; see bamboo
takeni-gusa; see plume poppy
takeshima-yuri; see lilium (3)
tamana; see kale
tamarisk — Tamarix chinensis Lour.—gyoryū
tangerine; see citrus
tani-watari; see asplenium
teika-kazura; see trachelospermum
temari-bana; see viburnum (2)
tenjiku-aoi; see geranium
tenjiku-botan; see dahlia
tenmondō; see asparagus
ten-nan-shō; see arisaema
teppō-yuri; see lilium (4)
tessen; see clematis
thermopsis — Thermopsis fabacea DC.—sendai-hagi
thistle — Cirsium japonicum DC.—azami
thoroughwort — Eupatorium stoechadosmum Hance —fuji-
hakama
tōgarashi; see capsicum
tōgoma; see castor-oil plant
tōhi; see spruce
tō-kinsen; see calendula
tokusa; see horsetail
tora-no-o; see lysimachia (1)
torch ginger — Amomum magnificum Benth. et Hook
tori-kabuto; see aconite
tori-tomarazu; see berberis
tō-tsubaki; see camellia (2)
trachelospermum — Trachelospermum asiaticum Nakai—teika-
tree peony — Paeonia suffruticosa Andr.—botan   ⌊kazura
tsubaki; see camellia (1)
tsuge; see box
tsukimi-sō; see oenothera
tsukinuki-nindō; see lonicera (2)
tsukubane-asagao; see petunia
tsuru-nichinichi-sō; see periwinkle
tsuru-umemodoki; see celastrus
tsuta; see Boston ivy
tsutsuji; see azalea (1)
tsuwa-buki; see ligularia (1)
tsuyu-kusa; see commelina
tuberose — Polianthes tuberosa L.—gekkakō (com. chuberōzu)
tulip — Tulipa Gesneriana L.—chūrippu

udo; see aralia   ⌈maki
umbrella pine — Sciadopitys verticillata Sieb. et Zucc.—kōya-
ume; see plum
umemodoki; see ilex (2)

u-no-hana; see deutzia
unzen-tsutsuji; see rhododendron (2)
urajiro; see gleichenia
utsubo-kazura; see pitcher plant
utsugi; see deutzia

vaccinium (blueberry) — Vaccinium ciliatum Thunb.—natsu-
variegated laurel; see aucuba   ⌊haze
verbena — Verbena phlogiflora Cham.—bijo-zakura
viburnum — (1) Viburnum dilatatum Thunb.—gama-zumi (2) V.
    tomentosum Thunb. (Japanese snowball)—temari-bana (com.
violet — Viola mandshurica W. Beck.—sumire   ⌊ōdemari)

warata; see waratah
waratah — Telopea speciosissima R. Br.—warata
waremokō; see sanguisorba (2)
water lily — (1) Nymphaea capensis Thunb. var. zanzibariensis
    Casp.—afurika suiren (com. suiren). (2) N. Marliacea Hort. var.
    chromatella Casp.—otoko-suiren (com. suiren). (3) N. rubra
    Roxb.—akabana hitsuji-gusa. (com. suiren). (4) N. tetragona
    Georgi var. angusta Casp. subvar. orientalis Casp.—hitsuji-gusa
    (com. suiren).
weeping willow — Salix babylonica L.—shidare-yanagi
white alder; see clethra
white birch — Betula Tauschii Koidz.—shira-kaba
wisteria — Wisteria floribunda DC.—noda-fuji (com. fuji)
wisteria vine — Wisteria floribunda DC.—fuji-zuru

yaguruma-giku; see cornflower
yaguruma-sō; see rodgersia
yakiba-zasa; see bamboo (3)
yama-bōshi; see cornus (2)
yamabuki; see kerria
yama-hagi; see bush clover
yama-momo; see myrica
yama-ran; see eupatorium
yama-tsutsuji; see azalea (1)
yama-yuri; see lilium (1)
yarrow — Achillea sibirica Ledeb.—nokogiri-sō or hagoromo-sō
yatsude; see fatsia
yellow day lily — Hemerocallis disticha Don—no-kanzō (com.
yellow iris; see iris (6)   ⌊kanzō)
yellow water lily — Nuphar japonicum DC.—kōhone
yoshi; see reed
yoshino-yuri; see lilium (1)
yoshi-take; see great reed
yuki-yanagi; see spiraea (3)
yusu; see distylium
yūzen-giku; see aster (4)

zakuro; see pomegranate
zeni-aoi; see mallow
zeranyūmu; see geranium
zinnia — Zinnia elegans L.—hyakunichi-sō

Bibliography

THIS BIBLIOGRAPHY lists publications that proved helpful to the author in the preparation of this book and is not necessarily intended as a suggested reading list. When a title is given in Japanese, followed by an English translation in parentheses, the book is in the Japanese language; all other books are in English.

Bailey, L. H.: *Standard Cyclopedia of Horticulture*. 3 vol. 1950.

Chittenden, Fred J. (ed.): *Dictionary of Gardening*. 4 vol. Royal Horticultural Society. 1951.

Dai Nippon Kadô-kai (ed.): *Kadô Kosho-Shûseisho* (Collections of Old Books on Flower Arrangement). 5 vol. 1931.

Fujiwara Yûchiku: *Ikenobô Ikebana Dokushûsho* (Ikenobô Ikebana Self-taught). 1957.

Heibonsha (pub.): *Sekai Daihyakka Jiten* (Encyclopedia of the World). 28 vol. 1957.

Hibonkaku (pub.): *Kadô Zenshû* (Complete Works of Japanese Flower Arrangement). 12 vol. 1935.

Ikenobô Sen'ei: *Ikenobô Ikebana* (Ikenobô Flower Arrangement). 1957.

Ikenobô Senkei (ed.): *Hana Kagami: Rikka Shiori-no-maki* (Guide to Rikka). 1911.

——: *Hana Kagami: Shôka Shiori-no-maki* (Guide to Shôka). 1904.

Koehn, Alfred: *Japanese Flower Symbolism*. 1954.

Makino Tomitarô: *Makino Nippon Shokubutsu Zukan* (Makino's Illustrated Flora of Japan, Enlarged Edition). 1957.

Murakoshi Michio: *Genshoku Shokubutsu Daizukan* (Flora in Color, Enlarged Edition). 5 vol. Revised by Makino Tomitarô. 1956.

Papinot, E.: *Dictionary—History and Geography of Japan*. 1927.

Sanders' Encyclopaedia of Gardening. Revised by A. G. L. Hellyer. 1956.

Shun-ô Chôsuian (pub.): *Hana-no-shiori* (Guide to Flowers). 1926.

Teshigahara Sôfû: *Sôgetsu-ryû Ikebana Dokushûsho* (Ikebana of the Sôgetsu School Self-taught). 1959.

Glossary and Index

A NUMBER of terms included here do not appear in the text itself and therefore are not followed by page references. They have been included for their possible reference value, particularly to persons who study with a Japanese teacher of flower arrangement. Plants are listed here only by the names used in the text; for alternate names in English and Japanese, see Appendix 2.

The following guide to the pronunciation of vowels in Japanese words may prove helpful: *a* as in "father"; *i* as in "machine"; *u* as in "put"; *û* (or *ū*) as in "rule"; *e* as in "ten"; *o* as in "solo"; and *ô* (or *ō*) as in "tone."